HOW TO
GROW
LEADERS

HOW TO GROW LEADERS

The seven key principles of effective leadership development

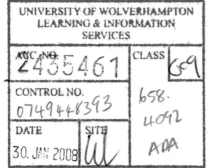

JOHN ADAIR

**KOGAN
PAGE**

London and Philadelphia

Publisher's note

Every possible effort has been made to ensure that the information contained in this book is accurate at the time of going to press, and the publishers and author cannot accept responsibility for any errors or omissions, however caused. No responsibility for loss or damage occasioned to any person acting, or refraining from action, as a result of the material in this publication can be accepted by the editor, the publisher or the author.

First published in Great Britain and the United States in 2005 by Kogan Page Limited
Reprinted 2005
Paperback edition 2007
Reprinted 2007

120 Pentonville Road
London N1 9JN
United Kingdom
www.kogan-page.co.uk

525 South 4th Street, #241
Philadelphia PA 19147
USA

© John Adair, 2005

The right of John Adair to be identified as the author of this work has been asserted by him in accordance with the Copyright, Designs and Patents Act 1988.

ISBN-10:   0 7494 4839 3
ISBN-13:   978 0 7494 4839 4

British Library Cataloguing-in-Publication Data

A CIP record for this book is available from the British Library.

Library of Congress Cataloging-in-Publication Data

Adair, John Eric, 1934–
  How to grow leaders: the seven key principles of effective leadership development/John Adair
      p. cm.
    ISBN 0-7494-4363-4
    1. Leadership. 2. Executives–Training of. 3. Executive ability. I. Title.
HD57.7.A2749 2005
658.4´092—dc22

2005002853

Typeset by Datamatics Technologies Ltd, Mumbai, India
Printed and bound in Great Britain by Creative Print and Design (Wales), Ebbw Vale

Contents

Changing things is central to leadership.
Changing them before anyone else is creative leadership.

Introduction

'Can you point us to an organization that is growing leaders?' they asked me. Silence fell in my room, and I gazed out of the window, reflecting.

At the time I was the world's first Professor of Leadership Studies, and so I suppose my two visitors to the university understandably expected me to know the answer. 'Not the armed forces,' they added, 'we have already been to see them.'

After a few minutes... well, I could think of plenty of companies that were *training* leaders – sending their first-line managers, for example, on action-centred leadership courses – but that was not the question they asked. Who is *growing* leaders?

'I cannot think of anyone,' I replied eventually.

'Alright then,' they said, 'we will do it. Will you help us?'

I agreed to do so, and they told me more about their situation. My visitors, Bill Stead and Edgar Vincent, were the senior group human resources managers in ICI, then known as 'the bellwether of British industry'. (A 'bellwether' is literally the leading sheep of a flock, the practice being to hang a bell around its neck.)

This particular bell was already tinkling the death knell of old-style management in the UK. Not that the rest of the flock had ears to hear it. In 1988, Bill and Edgar told me, the profits of ICI fell by a staggering 48 per cent; the dividend was cut for the first time since the formation of the company in 1926. ICI was too large (over 60,000 employees), too bureaucratic and in the wrong markets. The main board executive directors had decided that ICI's top priority was to develop *manager-leaders* – the first time, I recall, that I had ever heard that particular phrase.

Over the next five years we went about growing leaders in the nine divisions of ICI, but here let me 'cut to the chase'. *After five years ICI was the first British company in history to make a billion pounds profit.*

I tell you this story as they say 'up-front' in order to impress upon you that leadership is not a soft skill, an optional extra for oiling the machinery of industrial relations. It is a *key factor in business success* – whatever your business and however you define success.

The military learnt that lesson long ago. As the Greek poet Euripides, who died in 406 BCE, put it succinctly:

> Ten good soldiers wisely led,
> Will beat a hundred without a head.

Success in war or battle tends to go hand-in-hand with good leadership at all levels.

Leadership exists on three broad levels, which I named some time ago as *strategic, operational* and *team*, and that nomenclature is now beginning to catch on. It is a common fallacy that all an organization needs is a good strategic leader at the helm. The secret of business success is *excellence of leadership at all three levels.*

Organizations may be able to buy-in new strategic business leaders for astronomical salaries, like world-class football clubs changing their managers. But faced with the task of developing excellent leadership at *all* levels they have no option but to follow that distant bell of ICI in the 1980s and grow their own leaders.

In Part 1. Exploring Leadership, as that title suggests, I invite you to join me on a journey of discovery about the nature of leadership and how it can be taught.

My reasons are two-fold. First, unless you are reasonably clear what leadership is, and how it relates to management or command, you will be seriously handicapped when it comes to attempting to develop leadership. If you don't know what it is, how can you develop it?

Then we can get to work together in Part 2. How to Grow Leaders – The Seven Principles with *your* organization in mind. I can outline for you the principles, and clothe them as best I can in flesh and blood, but here you will be doing most of the thinking. For you know your fields of business and your particular organization, and only you know how to apply the principles in your context.

What you do with the knowledge you will glean from these pages does depend, of course, on your role. If you happen to be in the role of a principal strategic leader – say as chairman or chief executive – then you 'own the problem' of developing leaders. Or, strictly speaking, your organization or institution owns the problem and you need to ensure that it is addressing it in an effective and long-term way.

Alternatively, you may have the role in an organization – increasingly common now – that makes you a professional adviser to your colleagues in talent development matters, perhaps as head of personnel or human resources. Or you may be one of the growing number of consultants specializing in helping organizations to develop their leaders – a role that, in the language of theatre, I 'created' as Adviser in Leadership Training at the Royal Military Academy Sandhurst in the 1960s.

Before I begin, I should give you a brief historical overview. We are in the midst of a global revolution, moving fairly rapidly from old-style management to the concept of business leadership (using 'business' in its widest sense of what one is busy in). Leadership is now coming to be seen as existing on three broad levels: team, operational and strategic. I call this the 'leadership revolution'.

The origin of this revolution was my *Training for Leadership* (Macdonald & Jane, 1968), the world's first book on leadership development. In it I sowed the bean that would one day produce the true leadership revolution, namely the seminal idea that being a manager is but one form of being in the generic role of leader. That role I outlined for the first time in the book. Also in its pages I signposted the concept of the three levels of leadership, though only in my later books did I develop the idea.

It is not my intention to write here a history of the leadership revolution in the United States, where my work in the 1960s was ignored. Nor to comment upon the leadership industry that has now sprung up with its intellectual roots in the United States, and the laborious way that it is slowly reinventing the various wheels that I discovered in the 1960s. Others have done that, notably in *Leadership in Organizations: Current Issues and Key Trends* (Routledge, 2004), edited by John Storey, Professor of Human Resource Management at the Open University Business School.

This book is in the nature and style of a personal odyssey. Leadership grows by a natural process. I have sought to understand that natural way, and to advise organizations on how to work with the grain of nature rather than against it. In that journey I have tried to understand and draw upon my own experience of growing as a leader. Hence this book is the most personal and the most reflective of all my writings on the theme of leadership.

Yet I write too with a strong sense that my message is highly relevant. The world has moved on its axis. Never before have the climate and conditions been so opportune as they are today for organizations to embrace the practical philosophy and spirit of this book.

Plato said once: 'Those who have torches will hand them on to others.' In this book I am handing the torch to you. May it light the path forwards for you. May it help you to help others to grow as leaders. May it – if all else fails – be a star on your own personal journey towards excellence as a leader.

PART 1

Exploring Leadership – A Personal Odyssey

By the end of reading Part 1 you will have explored with me into the heart of leadership, following three uphill paths – the Qualities Approach (what a leader has to *be*), the Situational Approach (what a leader has to *know*), and the Group or Functional Approach (what a leader has to *do*). But we have no option to follow these paths separately: think of them as a whole. Not as a chemical mixture but as a compound.

Together they constitute nothing less than the generic role of *leader*. It is a discovery as significant in the social field as either Einstein's general theory of relativity in physics or Crick and Watson's double-helix structure of DNA in biology.

The proof of the pudding is in the eating. Putting that 1960s breakthrough in understanding the generic role of leadership – the integrated or composite theory I developed – to work in *selecting* and *training* leaders has proved to be spectacularly successful.

Ad fontes, 'To the fountains', was the motto of a famous English Renaissance scholar and medical doctor. Together in Part 1 we shall journey back in time to the very roots of modern thinking about leadership and how to grow leaders – Athens in the time of Socrates. Fasten your seatbelt!

1

The Qualities Approach

It was said that he had all the qualities of leadership which a man of his sort could have.

Xenophon

The highest-scoring British fighter ace in the Royal Air Force during World War II was Johnny Johnson. In his memoir *Wing Leader* (Chatto & Windus, 1956), he reveals the impact that the legendary legless Douglas Bader's leadership made upon him and his fellow young pilots in the early, hazardous days of the Battle of Britain. When Bader was eventually shot down (he became a prisoner of war), Johnson writes:

> At Tangmere we had simply judged Bader on his ability as a leader and a fighter pilot, and for us the high sky would never be the same again. Gone was the confident, eager, often scornful voice. Exhorting us, sometimes cursing us, but always holding us together in the fight. Gone was the greatest tactician of them all. Today marked the end of an era that was rapidly becoming a legend.
>
> *The elusive, intangible qualities of leadership can never be taught, for a man either has them or he hasn't.* Bader had them in full measure and on every flight had shown us how to apply them. He had taught us the true meaning of courage, spirit, determination, guts – call it what you will. Now that he was gone, it was our task to follow his signposts which pointed the way ahead.

Johnson was not alone in finding Bader such an inspiring example. In a letter to *The Times* (12 December 1996), the widow of another celebrated pilot, Hugh Dundas, who flew with Bader in 1940 and 1941, quoted from her husband's wartime letters to her about his commanding officer: 'He showed me quite clearly by his example the way in which a man should behave in time of war' and, 'Here was a man made in the mould of Francis Drake – a man to be followed, a man who would win.' Her husband, she continued, was aged 20 at the time, had been shot down a month before and viewed the prospect of combat with real inner fear. Bader's leadership and courage enabled him to continue flying Spitfires in action in Europe, and Bader remained a great and true friend until his death.

THE LONG SHADOW OF A TRUE LEADER

In later life Douglas Bader seized every opportunity to visit people, especially the young people who faced the trauma of amputations and the prospect of learning to walk again after leg amputations.

In August 2002 a racing car driver criminally knocked 36-year-old fireman Rob Green off his motorbike, killing his wife Lorna. Scarred by bad burns, Rob also lost both legs.

As the drugs wore off, he became terribly depressed. 'I felt so empty,' he says. 'I had lost everything; my beloved wife, the active life I had loved, my work – I wish I had died too. I never considered suicide, but I felt dying would have been much easier than living the life I had been left with.'

The final stage of his recovery was at a London hospital, where he spent three months learning to walk using artificial limbs. While learning to walk, Rob drew inspiration from the late Douglas Bader, the famous fighter ace who lost both his legs in a plane crash, but learnt to fly again.

'I'd seen a film about him before I lost my own legs. While in hospital I read his autobiography and it really helped me. One of his quotes which really spurred me on was "A disabled person who fights back is not disabled; they are inspired." It gave me courage to keep fighting.'

The sentence of Johnny Johnson's reminiscence that I have placed in italics above serves to introduce what I call the Qualities Approach to leadership and leadership development. It was virtually universal when I was born, the only horse in the race. Indeed, in that year (1934) Dr Hensley Henson, the Lord Bishop of Durham, gave a lecture on leadership to the University of St Andrews. He informed his audience:

> It is a fact that some men possess an inbred superiority which gives them a dominating influence over their contemporaries, and marks them out unmistakably for leadership. This phenomenon is as certain as it is mysterious. It is apparent in every association of human beings, in every variety of circumstances and on every plane of culture. In a school among boys, in a college among students, in a factory, shipyard, or a mine among the workmen, as certainly as in the Church and in the Nation, there are those who, with an assured and unquestioned title, take the leading place and shape the general conduct.

The assumption behind the Bishop's comments is both obvious and simple, an axiom that everyone took for granted. *Leaders are born and not made*; leadership consists of certain intrinsic traits or qualities that a person either has or has not.

The Qualities Approach certainly gave a strong answer to the most basic question in the field of the study of leadership: *Why is it that one person becomes the leader in a working group rather than another?* But it seemed to shut the door forever on young people like myself – conscious that we were not 'born leaders' but still wanting to be leaders.

How, if at all, could these 'qualities of leadership' be acquired? 'Smith is not a born leader yet,' said one school report. How could Smith be born again?

CAN LEADERSHIP QUALITIES BE DEVELOPED?

One overcast, rainy morning in 1897 a 12-year-old boy, Jafar Al-Askari, his brother and a soldier servant boarded a *kalak*, a native Iraqi river raft made of wood and inflated goatskins, and left Mosul in northern Iraq. As he narrates in *A Soldier's Story* (Arabian Publishing, 2003), Jafar and his companions sailed down the Tigris, passed Tikrit – home of a later and more infamous Iraqi leader – until seven days later they reached their destination. 'I enrolled in the Military School in Baghdad, and then later transferred to the Royal Military College in Constantinople [Istanbul]. There I was to graduate as an officer at the age of 19, when I was commissioned as a lieutenant in the Ottoman Army.' Later, in World War I, General Jafar Pasha – having changed sides – fought alongside T E Lawrence against the Turks for Arab independence, and later still he served no less than five times as prime minister of the newly-created Iraq.

On the College syllabus in the days of his youth Jafar comments in his memoirs: 'Our military education absolutely excluded any training in leadership qualities.' I doubt that in 1904 any other military academy in the world offered such training either, but it is interesting that Jafar clearly regarded it as an omission.

THE SECRET INGREDIENT

In the 1930s a Japanese naval officer cadet on a course at the Royal Britannia Naval College at Dartmouth was found by the orderly officer wandering around the corridors late at night with a notebook in hand.

'What are you doing?' he was asked.

'I am looking for the lectures on leadership,' replied the Japanese cadet. 'Obviously you give these lectures in the middle of the night so that we students from foreign countries should not be privileged to attend and learn about this subject which is so important to you.'

The belief that leadership qualities can and should be taught grew as time went by; what was less clear was how it should be done. The obvious approach seemed to be to list the constituent qualities and then to talk about each of them, with illustrations from the lives of great leaders.

An early example of the approach is a sixpenny self-help booklet published in 1912 in the UK entitled *How To Be a Leader of Others*, which I have on my table in front of me. The author begins:

There are in our midst today many undeveloped strong men: men who might, with proper training, have been leaders of others. Strong men, yet not quite strong enough to cause themselves to emerge from the crowd, and let their personalities have its full power. What such men as these need is just a little impetus – a fillip to their energies.

In order to arouse or excite this hidden leadership in the reader the anonymous author boldly identifies what he regards as the chief or distinguishing quality of a leader – *confidence*:

It would be difficult to find any group of men or women, or even boys or girls, that did not contain the one dominant spirit to whom it seems natural to assume command.

Such a one is always to be found, and such a one will always come to the front in a crisis, and will be ready to take the lead in a forlorn hope, in a game, or in mischief, or in organizing an expedition, a strike or a new movement. What is the gift that makes a person a successful leader of others?

It is simply confidence.

It means confidence in one's powers, and if that confidence is great enough and strong enough it will inspire others, and they will believe in the leader as firmly as he believes in himself, perhaps more so.

It is true that a successful leader will possess other characteristics in varying degrees such as 'pleasant social qualities which make him popular' or a 'fine and generous sympathy which enables him to understand human nature', but *confidence* is the most important, the one absolutely indispensable qualification. Now that is 'the whole secret of leadership, yet we often hear the expression "a born leader of men"'. Is it then necessary to be born with the gifts of leadership; can they not be acquired?

Alexander the Great, Dr Samuel Johnson, William Wallace, Attila the Hun and Wellington are then pressed into service as the 'object lessons' for leadership qualities, such as *ambition, courage, determination, energy, dignity, magnetism, coolness* and *self-discipline*. Contemporaries also commended as exemplars include the prime minister of the day Herbert Asquith, Joseph Chamberlain, Theodore Roosevelt, Lord Kitchener, Admiral Lord Beresford and (rather oddly to our eyes) Kaiser Wilhelm

II – 'a strong-willed and inspiring leader, able to secure the affection and obedience of his subjects'.

My personal encounter with the Qualities Approach came in 1953, when I was conscripted into the British Army to do what was then called National Service. The officer training course had only one period of instruction on leadership. It consisted of a talk on the 'qualities of leadership'. The summer afternoon was warm and we had been on a patrolling exercise the night before, so I remember nodding off to sleep. But we were issued with a handout or précis, which I still have.

It begins by asking, 'What is leadership?' and – in military style – tells you the 'Directing Staff' answer, so there is no need to do any thinking for yourself:

> It is the art of influencing a body of people to follow a certain course of action; the art of controlling them, directing them and getting the best out of them. A major part of leadership is Man-Management.

Leadership is then broken down into no less than 17 qualities, each with a sentence or two of explanation:

- Ability to make decisions
- Energy
- Humour
- Sense of justice
- Determination
- Example
- Physically fit
- Pride in command
- Loyalty
- Sense of duty
- Calmness in crisis
- Assurance (confidence)
- Ability to accept responsibility
- Human element
- Initiative
- Resolute courage
- Enthusiasm

Quite how – if at all – one could develop these qualities that make a good leader was not indicated. Experience seemed to be the only doorway. 'Never imagine that you have learnt all about leadership,' the handout concluded. 'You will always have something more to learn, so be prepared to profit by experience. Experience helps a great deal. Take every opportunity of gaining experience in leadership.'

As we were all about to become platoon commanders, to many of us like myself in 'active service' situations, this last piece of advice might have seemed a bit superfluous!

It is difficult to acquire qualities or virtues as if by frontal assault with one's willpower. Actually the officer cadet in the bed next to me did try to develop the 17 qualities in this way. He took three each day, I recall, as the daily quota. On Wednesdays, for example, he tried to acquire a sense of humour by laughing at the cartoons in *Punch* – which struck me as a rather serious way of going about it! At the end of the week he either thought he had all of the 17 qualities in abundant measure, which made him pretty well impossible to live with; or he concluded that he was more or less devoid of not only these qualities but others as well. That tended to remove what was left of his self-confidence. He soon abandoned it as a hopeless enterprise.

Ten years later the British Army, through my influence, introduced a totally new and revolutionary approach to leadership training. Without abandoning the Qualities Approach – wisely, as time showed – Sandhurst adopted the Group or Functional Approach. But that merits a chapter of its own.

2

The Group or Functional Approach

On a journey, the leader of the people is their servant.
                                    The Prophet Muhammad

Sandhurst is not the first place most people would think of as a source of ideas on human relations. Indeed, academic prejudice against the Services is strong enough to ensure that the opportunities they offer for the detailed study of individuals and groups in action are underrated, if not ignored, by sociologists and others.

So begins a book review by Donald McLachlan, editor of *The Sunday Telegraph*, writing in 1968. He continues:

Nonetheless John Adair, who lectures on military history and advises on leadership training at the Royal Military Academy Sandhurst, has written in *Training for Leadership* the first book known to me which tries to break down the meaning of the word leadership, and to discover ways in which the military business of leading can be taught with modern educational techniques.

I say 'business' because at its simplest a leader's task is to get a difficult job done well, quickly and willingly – even enjoyably. There are other aspects depending on the situation in which leadership is called for: courage in defeat, inspiration in apathy, clarity of mind in confusion – but the basic requirement is that the led should understand the task, trust the leader and know how to do what is required.

Leadership, therefore, is to an extent not generally admitted, a skill which can be learnt: and Dr Adair has devised ways of showing cadets what is required of a man giving orders to a group, whether a lieutenant with a company or a foreman on a production line.

With breezy ruthlessness Dr Adair brushes aside what he calls 'the qualities approach' to leadership instruction. You take the characteristics of great commanders and then hope the pupils will follow their examples. How unsatisfactory this is is shown by the lists of leadership qualities compiled in different institutions.

Our own Naval College at Dartmouth puts at the top Faith and after it Knowledge; but the RAF college rates Efficiency first and Personality second. (Even allowing for historical differences, the disparity is astonishing.) The US Army puts Bearing first and Courage second, whereas the US Marine Corps starts with Integrity and ranks Knowledge second. Field Marshal Slim – a leader if ever there was one – rates Courage highest and after it Willpower.

Even more disturbing is the fact that the list of qualities runs to 15 at Dartmouth, seven at Cranwell, 14 in the US Marine Corps – and that only the Canadian Military College includes Humour.

Dr Adair understandably finds this state of affairs unacceptable and in his clear, modest and carefully argued book shows the way to a closer analysis.

We are left free to continue speculation and rhapsody about the qualities that kept Bomber Command flying to Berlin, gave the Eighth Army its identity, and imparted to the Mediterranean Fleet its dash. But we are also strengthened in our feeling that to distrust the word itself, because it was abused by a Duce and a Fuehrer, and to underrate the quality, is bad for a democratic society.

Donald McLachlan captured in his article the nature of the revolution in thinking about leadership and leadership training that had unfolded at Sandhurst during the 1960s. Even though that revolution triggered off in turn the leadership revolution of today, incidentally the 'academic prejudice' that McLachlan mentioned then persists to this day. US academics in this field are completely parochial, and also intellectually at sea; British and European academics have tended to follow them like sheep on their wanderings.

WHAT IS THE GROUP OR FUNCTIONAL APPROACH?

> Not much smaller than the bibliography on leadership is the diversity of views on the topic. Even a cursory review of these investigations shows that leadership means many different things to different people. Far from being a unitary concept or simple dimension, it is probably one of the most complex phenomena social psychology offers.

So wrote the two US authors, J W Thibaut and H H Kelley in *The Social Psychology of Groups* (McGraw-Hill, 1959). They added that an 'understanding of leadership must rest on a more basic understanding of the structure and functioning of groups'.

By 1959, as I shall describe later, the Group or Functional Approach was already in use in Britain – it was formulated in a rough form and applied successfully in selecting military leaders in the British Army from 1941 onwards, continuously. Not until the 1960s, however, did I formulate the complete theory of that 'more basic understanding of the structure and functioning of groups' which Thibaut and Kelley correctly stipulated as the necessary condition for understanding leadership. In a nutshell it is as follows.

All working groups, provided they have been together for some time, develop what I call a *group personality* (a phrase that was originally used by Clement Attlee about Cabinets). Yet the other side of the coin is that they also have present in them *group needs*. These are common or universal, in the sense that all working groups have them. They are:

■ the need to achieve the common task;
■ the need to be held together or maintained as a working unity;
■ the needs which individuals bring into them by virtue of being embodied persons.

The next step is to say that these three areas of need are not separate or static – they are interactive and dynamic. It was the great breakthrough to perceive this interrelation as three overlapping circles (shown in Figure 2.1). A lot of leadership is common sense, but no amount of common sense could have produced this model – it required an inspired or creative moment.

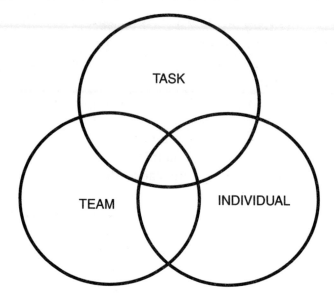

Figure 2.1   The three areas of need

My version substituted *team* for the original *group (needs)*. In the Sandhurst context 'team' sounded less like jargon than 'group needs'. It proved to be a correct decision.

The functions of leadership

In order to meet the three areas of need certain *functions* have to be performed, such as *planning* or *controlling*. A function is what you do, as opposed to a quality, which is what you are. From the Latin *functio*, performance, a function is one of a group of related actions contributing to a larger action – in this instance the meeting of the Three Circles.

The key functions required are more or less as follows. I say 'more or less' because diligent readers of my books will notice some variations in the lists. I don't think this really matters – a fixed orthodox list would ossify what should be living material. Here is my original Sandhurst list:

■ *Planning*   Seeking all available information.

Defining group task, purpose or goal.

Making a workable plan (in right decision-making framework).

■ *Initiating*   Briefing group on the aims and the plan.

Explaining why aim or plan is necessary.

Allocating tasks to group members.

Setting group standards.

■ *Controlling*   Maintaining group standards.

Influencing tempo.

Ensuring all actions are taken towards objectives.

Prodding group to action/decision.

■ *Supporting*   Expressing acceptance of persons and their contribution.

Encouraging group/individuals.

Disciplining group/individuals.

Creating team spirit.

Reconciling disagreements or getting others to explore them.

■ *Informing*   Clarifying task and plan.

Giving new information to the group, ie keeping them 'in the picture'.

Receiving information from the group.

Summarizing suggestions and ideas coherently.

■ *Evaluating*   Checking feasibility of an idea.

Testing the consequences of a proposed solution.

Evaluating group performance.

Helping the group to evaluate its own performance.

In the Group or Functional Approach as developed by me these functions are clearly labelled *leadership* functions. Here *function* refers to activity demanded by one's position, profession or the like; the proper or characteristic action of a person in a given role.

That doesn't mean to say that the designated leader should perform all these functions himself or herself. Indeed the theory suggests that it is impossible. In groups of more than three or four people there are just too many actions classifiable under the functions that are required to meet the requirements of task, team and individual for any one person to do them. But the leader is accountable for the three circles. Taken together these functions constitute the *generic role of leader*.

The distinctive hallmarks of the theory are the three-factor Three Circles model, the concepts of a single set of functions meeting the whole, and the clear identification of them as *leadership* functions in the sense of being the prime responsibility of the designated leader.

In these respects the Group or Functional Approach was streets ahead of its time in the 1960s. It falls outside the scope of this book to set it against the contemporary US social psychological theories about leadership, or the quite separate path of evolution since 1959. The US carpet-bombing of leadership continued – some 40,000 books (over 10,000 still in print) and over 10,000 research studies – but without removing that underlying confusion which Thibaut and Kelley had noted in 1959. In the long race since 1934 to discover the generic role of leader, it was a British thinker who achieved the breakthrough.

APPLYING THE GROUP OR FUNCTIONAL APPROACH TO TRAINING

No theory is credible until it is applied to practice – and works. Moreover, it has to work in many different conditions and over a sustained period of time.

The first major trial in the 1960s involved using the new philosophy in the *training* of military leaders at Sandhurst and in the Royal Air Force and Royal Navy – over 5,000, together with a smaller sample of several hundred junior managers in companies like Wates, Wilson Connolly Holdings and Dorothy Perkins. While that work was in progress, however, I became aware that, as mentioned above, a prototype had already been applied during World War II to *selecting* leaders with equal and continuing success.

Having identified the role and functions of leadership it now became possible for the first time ever to *train* people to be team leaders. At Sandhurst this training was kick-started with a concentrated one and a half-day course, which I designed and tested. It then continued in what I called 'Field Leadership Training'. As its name implies, whenever an officer cadet occupied a leadership role during tactical exercises in the field there was a 'debriefing' afterwards which covered *both* tactical *and* leadership performance. The latter was conducted on a discussion basis, using the Three Circles model and the set of key functions like a compass. Not least by acting as observers and teachers of their peers in this way – quite apart from what they learnt by having a chance at leading themselves – the officer cadets grew as effective leaders and team members.

Training for Leadership (Macdonald & Jane, 1968) was my write-up of this revolution at Sandhurst and elsewhere. On the strength of it another distinguished Spitfire ace of World War II, Neil Cameron (later Marshal of the Royal Air Force Lord Cameron and Chief of the Defence Staff), convened the first conference on leadership training to be held in the UK in 1967. One of the contributors, Harold Bridger, a psychologist at the Tavistock Institute who had served as a selector during the war, made a quiet remark that stuck in my mind: *The seeds of the future lie in the present.*

The Group or Functional Approach was an immense step forwards. It became the centrepiece of the whole Sandhurst training of military leaders. The Academy's motto, 'Serve to Lead' now became intelligible. It didn't mean that a young officer had to learn to obey orders himself before he could issue them to others with authority, though philosophers from Aristotle to Hegel had argued that such an experience for any leader is highly desirable: being on the receiving end teaches you a lot of lessons.

No, *serve* meant to meet those three interlocking areas of need, and to do so primarily by example – by leading from the front. A young officer had to acquire the knowledge and the qualities so that – although *appointed* – he would be accepted as the natural leader by his soldiers.

You can be appointed a commander or manager, but you are not a leader until your appointment is ratified in the hearts and minds of those who work under you.

In order to equip a young officer for the role of military leader, much more than specific training for leadership – such as I have been describing – is required. In *Training for Leadership* I talked about all those other elements – the ethos and tradition, the example of the staff, both officers and NCOs, the impact of military history, etc. It is a solemn but exciting moment when the newly commissioned officer at the Sovereign's Parade stands on the threshold of his or her career as a leader. In June 1966 the Queen addressed these words to them:

Today, those of you in the Senior Division become officers and it will not be long before those in the other Divisions follow in your steps. The day on which you receive your Commission is one of the most important in your life, because your duties and responsibilities as leaders of men are among the most onerous your country can confer upon you.

You have learnt here that an officer must be, above all else, a leader; a person whom men will follow into danger, discomfort and every ordeal which nature, climate or a human enemy can contrive. Remember always that the best and purest form of leadership is example; that 'Come on' is a much better command that 'Go on'.

You come of races renowned for courage and I know that as officers you will never fail to be the first in danger. But leadership in the stress and excitement of battle will not be your only responsibility. Your patience, inspiration and attention to detail will also be required in the often equally testing routine duties and in what may seem uneventful and even unimportant periods of service. These times call for leadership of a special kind if you are to keep the morale and efficiency of your men at the pitch required.

Leadership demands a dedicated responsibility towards the men under your command. Their lives will be in your hands and they will have the right to expect from you the highest standards of character, professional competence and integrity. If you will always put their interests and welfare before your own, you will not fail them and together you will be able to undertake any enterprise.

You will often inspect your men, I suspect that when you are doing so they will be just as keenly inspecting you.

Soldiers have always been ambassadors and representatives of their country. This applies with even greater force to officers. Your civilian countrymen will – perhaps unconsciously – pay you the compliment of expecting you to show, not only a higher degree of courage and duty than themselves, but, when serving abroad, a standard of behaviour which reflects well upon your country.

As you join your Units, you will be stepping into a profession which has played a most important and distinguished part in the evolution of this country. I am confident that you will continue to uphold its tradition as servant and protector of the state.

The path on which you are now setting out will often be rough and steep; my trust, my thoughts and my good wishes go with you on it.

In 1962 the Adjutant General was so alarmed at the poor standards of leadership among junior officers that he directed every unit in the British Army to hold a study day on the subject. The revolutionary improvements at Sandhurst changed that dismal picture. In the decades since the Queen gave that speech the Services have been almost constantly on active service – Northern Ireland, the Falklands, Bosnia, Iraq, and so on. Nothing is perfect, but in military leadership the Services has proved to be second to none. That is a source of pride to me, but there is also a great challenge to keep it that way. Like freedom, the price of good leadership is eternal vigilance.

3

Leaders or Managers?

We are going to win and the industrial West is going to lose: there is nothing much you can do about it, because the reasons for your failure are within yourselves.

'Your firms are built on the Taylor model; even worse, so are your heads. With your bosses doing the thinking while the workers wield the screwdrivers, you're convinced deep down that this is the right way to run a business.

Konosuke Matsushita, Tokyo 1979

In February 1983 the Harvard Business School announced that Abraham Zaleznik had been appointed to fill the Konosuke Matsushita Professorship of Leadership, the chair to be established 'to support research and teaching on the development of effective leadership in society' at Harvard. It was inaugurated in Japan in November 1981, some two years after I had taken up my appointment as the world's first Professor of Leadership Studies in the UK.

Zaleznik had come to notice in 1977 with an article in the *Harvard Business Review* entitled 'Managers and leaders: are they different?' (reprinted in 1992). Here a characteristically US dichotomy between 'leadership' and 'management' was advanced graphically and influentially. 'It takes neither genius nor heroism to be a manager,' he wrote, 'but rather persistence, tough-mindedness, hard work, intelligence, analytical ability and perhaps most important, tolerance and goodwill.' With that article as a symbolic starting line a huge consultancy industry developed around the notion of *not* 'managers' but 'leaders'.

Maybe, some said, organizations need both leaders and managers. Zaleznik would have none of that:

> It is easy enough to dismiss the dilemma... by saying that there is a need for people who can be both. But, just as a managerial culture differs from the entrepreneurial culture that develops when leaders appear in organizations, managers and leaders are very different kinds of people. They differ in motivation, personal history and in how they think and act.
> (Zaleznik, A, *Harvard Business Review*, 1992: 127)

In this black-and-white dichotomy, leaders 'think about goals, they are active rather than reactive, shaping ideas rather than responding to them'. Managers, by contrast, aim to 'shift balances of power towards solutions acceptable as compromises, managers act to limit choices, leaders develop fresh approaches'.

This controversy about the essential differences between leadership and management would fuel a thousand conferences. In fact it has proved to be a wild goose chase, for it begged the question as to whether or not there *is* an essential difference between a leader and a manager. It was the failure to think clearly enough about leadership that initially gave rise to the confusion, one from which there are a few signs that the academics are just beginning to emerge. The road has led them back to the general theory or philosophy that I propounded in *Training for Leadership* (Macdonald & Jane, 1968) and have been developing ever since.

DISCOVERING THE GENERIC ROLE OF LEADER

Only now, after 40 years have elapsed, can we appreciate the breakthrough of discovering the generic role of leader – symbolized by the Three Circles – in the 1960s. I compare it to a scientific discovery. The key passage in my 1968 book was as follows:

> Essentially leadership lies in the provision of the functions necessary for a group to achieve its task and be held together as a working team. Now this is basic, the raw 'silver' called leadership, which to some extent may be separated and analysed in functional terms. But in reality leadership always appears in a particular form or 'vessel' which can

be distinguished from others. The shape is fashioned above all by the *characteristic working situation* of the group or its parent organization…
In the military *milieu* the shape which leadership assumes is best called 'Command'; in the industrial and commercial situation it is known as 'Management'. Two boughs from the same tree, they can easily – but should not be – confused.

The philosopher Hegel once pointed out that one cannot eat *fruit* – it is only possible to eat *apples, grapes, pears, raspberries,* etc. By that analogy, *command* in the military field, *management* in various civilian fields, and *ministry* in the churches, are specific fruits – but leadership is *fruit*.

As the Chinese proverb says, 'It does not matter if a cat is black or white, as long as it catches mice.' The Group or Functional Approach, as I developed it, gave commanders, managers or ministers a clear idea of what they needed to *do* as occupants of the generic role of leader. Whether it was to be called 'management' or 'leadership' was, strictly speaking, an issue of semantics and secondary in importance.

The source of the confusion

How you may wonder, has all this confusion about leadership and management arisen? Oddly enough, there is a very simple explanation and the real culprit is the English language.

Take a look at *leadership* again. The *leader* part presents no problems, as I was the first to point out that it derives from the old Anglo-Saxon noun *laed* which means a path, road, way, or course of a ship at sea – it is a journey word. Actually it is that suffix, *-ship,* which has caused all the problems, for it has two broad senses in English.

Exercise

Look at the four senses of *-ship* in English given below and see if you can reduce them to two general ones:

- Official position, status or rank, such as *ambassadorship, citizenship, headship, professorship,* etc.
- Collective members of a group, as *membership* or *township*.

- Quality, state or condition, as *companionship, friendship, hardship, relationship*, etc.
- Skill or expertise in a certain capacity, as *craftsmanship, entrepreneur-ship, horsemanship*.

My solution to the exercise is that there are two general senses, which I liken to the heads and tails of a coin:

- *Heads* – *having* the position or dignity of leader, as in the *lead-ership* of the Trade Union Congress or the Arab world.
- *Tails* – the state or condition of *being* what is expressed by the substantive, the qualities or character associated with it or the power implied by it, as in 'he achieved great things by his *leadership* alone'.

Thus leadership is both *role* and *attribute*. The integrated theory or philosophy I developed at Sandhurst is the only one that integrates the heads and tails of leadership. Put simply, the Group or Functional Approach in the complete three-factor or triangular form gives us the *role*; the Qualities and Situational Approach (see the following chapter) gives us – together with functional skills – the *attribute*.

REVISITING THE QUALITIES APPROACH

In his review of *Training for Leadership* Donald McLachlan commented upon the 'breezy ruthlessness' with which I 'brushed aside' the Qualities Approach. Certainly for the purposes of the initial training of young leaders that is true, but the Qualities Approach remained in the frame: it was always part of the integrated theory. It does matter what you *are* as a leader. My early distinction between *representative* and *generic* qualities has also stood the test of time:

Representative

Leaders tend to exemplify or even personify *the qualities required or expected in the working group in question*. In the example of Douglas Bader, given in Chapter 1, actually all fighter pilots needed 'courage, spirit, determination, guts – call it what you will'. For *courage* is a military virtue, and as such is required in all combatants. What a military leader does is to exemplify it, and make it visible.

You can apply this principle to any field: nurses, teachers, lawyers, engineers, accountants, academics or research scientists. A leader should possess and express in his or her working life the four or five qualities that are perceived to be as essential in a good practitioner in that field.

Generic

There are some generic – across the board – attributes or qualities of leaders. My list includes:

- *Enthusiasm.* Can you think of any leader who lacks enthusiasm? It is hard to do so. It may be a quiet and slow-burning enthusiasm rather than the heat and fireworks of passion, but it is always there.
- *Integrity* – the quality that engenders trust. Why is it so important for leadership? 'Trust being lost,' wrote the Roman historian Livy, 'all the social intercourse of men is brought to naught.'
- *Toughness or' demandingness', coupled with fairness.* Leadership is not a popularity contest. People respect a leader with high standards who will not compromise on them, provided he or she is consistent, fair and does not ask from others what they do not require from themselves first.
- *Humanity.* 'Cold fish' do not make good leaders. Leaders need to exemplify basic humaneness, an inner kindness or sympathy when occasion calls for it.
- *Confidence.* No leader can operate without a quiet confidence. Confidence should not be confused with over-confidence. Indeed, without a level of self-confidence none of us could put our talents to work. Therefore leaders are not so unique in this respect.
- *Humility.* The result of having a proper sense of one's own limitations. Its hallmarks are a readiness to listen and to be taught, a willingness to admit when one is wrong, and a reverence for others.
- *Courage.* Whereas not all physically brave individuals have moral courage, all those with moral courage are physically brave as

well. Courage of either kind is universally admired, not least in a
leader.

In *Effective Leadership* (Pan, 1983) I demonstrated the *functional* value
or relevance in the context of the Three Circles model. In other words,
the natural integration of the Qualities Approach and the Group or
Functional Approach had advanced by then, like two paths with very
different starting points coming closer together as they draw nearer
to a mountain summit.

You may notice that I am adamant about *enthusiasm* and *integrity* as
generic leadership qualities, and then I become less sure as I go down
my provisional list, eventually tailing off. There are two reasons.

First, it is important to keep leadership open-ended, so that it is fun
to think about it and explore it. Cut-and-dried lists of 'essential qualities' (these days called 'leadership competencies') kill off thought.
Moreover, there just isn't the evidence to sustain more than two, three
or four generic qualities.

Secondly, the merit of keeping the list as short as possible is that
you don't over-burden leaders with false expectations, making them
feel secretly guilty all the time that they are not *really* leaders.

Here we need to apply a form of Occam's Razor to the post-
Zaleznik school who expect leaders to be heroic, transformational or
inspirational figures. William of Occam, a great medieval Franciscan
scholar, held that 'No more things should be presumed to exist then
are absolutely necessary.' It reminds us that all unnecessary facts or
constituents in a subject should be eliminated. In this context, we
should eliminate – or rather put on the optional list – all but the essentials of qualities, knowledge or skills. It is a help if a leader has a *sense
of humour* or consummate *tact*, for example, but it is not essential. But
if a leader lacks *enthusiasm* or *integrity* he or she is in danger of being
merely a tenant of their role, not a natural freeholder.

Do you have to be *inspirational* as a leader? This is a hard question
to answer because *inspirational* is one of the most frequently mentioned overtones of being a (good) leader. The answer is quite complex, but in simple terms inspiration is not a property of personality
or character. It is a phenomenon, like a rainbow. There has to be a con-
juncture of factors or circumstances to produce that phenomenon and
– like the rainbow – it comes and goes. The factors lie in the nature of

the *task*, the greatness of people in the *team*, and the fire inside the *leader*. When these planets align, then everyone – including the leader – experiences inspiration. (See my book, *The Inspirational Leader*, Kogan Page, 2003.)

THE MANAGER AS LEADER

In any field it takes a long time for conceptual or scientific break-throughs to become popular truisms, and – globally – there is a long journey ahead.

The false dichotomy between 'leaders' and 'managers' in the USA is now almost on its last legs. Also on the way out at last is the absurd notion that organizations need 'leaders' at the top and a staff of 'managers' at all levels below them – a modern form of Plato's class distinction between kings and philosophers (leaders), guardians (managers) and workers/slaves. It was one earlier form of that – Taylorism – that Matsushita criticized at the head of this chapter.

What we now know is that – whether they know it or not – managers are in the generic role of leader. As in the case of DNA, we have a map: it isn't a double helix, however, but what the mathematicians call a Venn diagram. It is simple, but it is also – again in the language of mathematics – deep.

The issue is really whether or not the management of a company are leaders. They are the leadership (role). The issue is whether or not they have leadership (attribute). The first thing you have to check, however, is if they do actually know what the *role* is. A surprising number of managers are still victims of tunnel vision: they see a narrow range of *task* functions and no more. Don't ever criticize a manager for not being a leader if no one has ever told him or her what the role is. Rather criticize the inept organization that appointed them. I hope I am not treading on your toes.

It all comes down to the basic question: *what are you being paid to do*? What we *call* the answer – leadership or management or something else – doesn't matter.

4

The Situational Approach

There is a small risk a leader will be regarded with contempt by those he leads if, whatever he may have to preach, he shows himself best able to perform.

Xenophon

The natural sequence (see my other books) is Qualities, Situational and Group or Functional Approaches. Here I am changing the order for a reason. Although the modern form of the Situational (*alias* Contingency) Approach was known in the 1960s in the writings of psychologists, it was not until long after I had left Sandhurst that I tracked down the true source of it, and thereby accidentally discovered what has proved to be a kind of Tutankhamun's Tomb. It is the second great discovery in my personal odyssey.

WHAT IS THE SITUATIONAL APPROACH?

Recall that basic question in our field: *why is it that one person in a group is perceived to be and accepted as the leader*? The answer of the Situational Approach is that *it all depends on the situation*.

Stogdill, for example, who studied the evidence for 29 qualities appearing in 124 studies, concluded that although intelligence, scholarliness, dependability, social participation and socio-economic status were found to bear some relation to leadership:

the evidence suggests that leadership is a relationship that exists between persons in a social situation, and that persons who are leaders in one situation may not necessarily be leaders in other situations.

(Ralph Stogdill, Ohio State University Press, 1948)

Another study by W O Jenkins, published a year earlier in 1947, supports this conclusion. After reviewing 74 studies on military leadership the author wrote:

Leadership is specific to the particular situation under investigation. Who becomes the leader of a particular group engaging in a particular activity and what the leadership characteristics are in the given case are a function of the specific situation. There are wide variations in the characteristics of individuals who become leaders in similar situations and even great divergence in leadership behaviour in different situations. The only common factor appeared to be that leaders in a particular field need and tend to possess superior general or technical competence or knowledge in that area. General intelligence does not seem to be the answer...

(W O Jenkins, 'A review of leadership studies with particular reference to military problems', *Psychological Bulletin*, 1947)

To illustrate this theory let us imagine some shipwreck survivors on a tropical island. The soldier in the party might take command if natives attacked them, the builder lead during the work of erecting houses, and the farmer might direct the labour of growing food. In other words, leadership would pass from member to member according to the situation. 'Situation' in this context means primarily the task of the group.

There are two drawbacks to this approach as far as training leaders is concerned. First, it is unsatisfactory in most organizations for leadership to change hands in this manner. At one time the Royal Air Force veered towards this doctrine by entertaining the idea that if a bomber crashed in a jungle the officer who took command for the survival operation might not be captain of the aircraft but the man most qualified for the job. But role flexibility to this degree tends to create more problems than it solves.

Secondly, an explanation was needed for the fact that certain men seemed to possess a general leadership competence that enabled them to exercise an influence over their fellows in a whole range of situations. Of course, the compilers of trait lists had been seeking, without much success, to analyse this general aptitude, and there was no denying its reality. Even so, by seeing leadership not as a quality but as a relationship, and *by grasping the importance of the leader possessing the appropriate technical or professional knowledge required in the given situation*, the proponents of this approach made a most valuable contribution to our understanding of the subject.

THE ORIGINS OF THE SITUATIONAL APPROACH

The Situational Approach, as I called it, actually dates back to Socrates in 5th-century BCE Athens. You may wonder how I can say that, given the fact that Socrates wrote no books. The answer is that two of his circle did write books: Plato and Xenophon. As they both wrote their various works in the form of Socratic dialogues, that is, between one or more interlocutors and Socrates, it is not easy to determine whether the voice we hear is that of Socrates on the one hand or the voices of Plato and Xenophon on the other. But as the kernel of the Situational Approach to understanding leadership – namely, that *in any situation people will tend to follow or obey the man or woman who knows what to do and how to do it* – is found in both Plato and Xenophon and attributed to their master, it is a sound surmise that it goes back to Socrates himself.

Both use the example of a ship's captain and his crew. Here is Plato's version from the *Republic*:

> The sailors are quarrelling over the control of the helm... they do not understand that the genuine navigator can only make himself fit to command a ship by studying the seasons of the year, sky, stars and winds, and all that belongs to his craft; and they have no idea that, along with the science of navigation, it is possible for him to gain, by instruction or practice, the skill to keep control of the helm whether some of them like it or not.

The case of the young cavalry commander

One day, Xenophon tells us, Socrates engaged in discussion with a newly elected cavalry commander in the Athenian Army. As Xenophon himself was elected to that office at the age of 23 or 24, it is tempting to believe that this is a piece of autobiography and that he is describing here his first encounter with 'The Thinker', as the young men called their intellectual mentor and beloved friend.

Under questioning from Socrates, the young man agreed that his seeking of the rank of commander could not have been because he wanted to be first in the cavalry charge, for, as Socrates pointed out, the mounted archers usually rode ahead of the commander into battle. Nor could it have been simply in order to get himself known by everyone – even madmen, he conceded under questioning from Socrates, could achieve that. He accepted Socrates' suggestion that it must have been because he wanted to leave the Athenian cavalry in better condition than when he found it. Xenophon, later both the world's first authority on horsemanship and the author of a textbook on commanding cavalry, had no difficulty in explaining what needs to be done to achieve that end. The young commander, for example, must improve the quality of the cavalry mounts; he must school new recruits – both horses and men – in equestrian skills and then teach the troopers their cavalry tactics. All these points emerged step by step out of the dialogue:

> 'And have you considered how to make the men obey you?' continued Socrates. 'Because without that, horses and men, however good and gallant, are of no use.'
>
> 'True, but what is the best way of encouraging them to obey, Socrates?' asked the young man.
>
> 'Well, I suppose you know that under all conditions human beings are most willing to obey those whom they believe to be the best. Thus in sickness they most readily obey the doctor, on board ship the pilot, on a farm the farmer, whom they think to be the most skilled in his business.'
>
> 'Yes, certainly,' said his student.
>
> 'Then it is likely that in horsemanship too, one who clearly knows best what ought to be done will most easily gain the obedience of the others.'

Xenophon captures here that very distinct theme in Socrates' teaching on leadership already identified above. In harmony with the rest of his practical philosophy of life and politics (for, despite his pose of ignorance, Socrates had ideas of his own), it emphasizes the importance of knowledge in leadership. People will obey willingly only those whom they perceive to be better qualified or more knowledgeable than themselves in a particular situation.

At the age of 26 years Xenophon accepted an invitation from his friend Proxenus to join him as what we would call a 'gentleman volunteer' on a military expedition to Babylon. A claimant to the Persian throne had hired a Greek army of 10,000 mercenaries. Proxenus was one of the six generals, but the senior one was a Spartan called Cleachus. Unfortunately they and their employer lost the critical battle: he lost his life and they were in danger of being made slaves. But under Cleachus' influence the Greeks decided to march 800 miles through enemy territory to the Black Sea and freedom. Not long after setting out the Persians treacherously murdered the six Greek generals. Xenophon was one of those elected to replace them, and he soon emerged as the commander-in-chief. He later wrote a famous account of the Persian expedition – they got to the sea in the end – in which, for the first time in history, the leadership of commanders is described. And, of course, Xenophon tells us how he put into practice the lessons he had learnt at the feet of Socrates.

Xenophon on leadership

At the head of Chapter 1, I quoted Xenophon's brief description of the Spartan general Cleachus. 'It was said that he had all the qualities of leadership which a man of his sort could have,' said Xenophon. It is evidently not a judgement that Xenophon shared, though clearly he held the Spartan (as he did all Spartans) in the highest respect. Yet Cleachus lacked something in his makeup – perhaps as a result of the narrow military upbringing that produced 'a man of his sort' – that made him fall short of the ideal of a leader that Xenophon had formed in his discussions with Socrates.

Make no mistake, Cleachus was a copybook example of one principal strand of the Socratic theory of leadership. When the army found itself in a crisis his unrivalled professional knowledge and experience stood out like a beacon and attracted men to him. As Xenophon writes:

> On these occasions, they said that his forbidding look seemed posi-
> tively cheerful, and his toughness appeared as confidence in the face of
> the enemy, so that it was no longer toughness to them but something
> to make them feel safe. On the other hand, when the danger was over
> and there was a chance of going away to take service under someone
> else, many of them deserted him, since he was invariably tough and
> savage, so that the relations between his soldiers and him were like
> those of boys to a schoolmaster.

Xenophon's last point, that Cleachus treated his soldiers like a peda-
gogue (literally in Greek a 'leader of children') is illuminating. The
Greeks prided themselves on the belief that they were the most intelligent people on the face of the earth; they were deeply conscious, too,
of their tradition of equality and democracy. Even when serving as
mercenary soldiers they did not like being bullied or treated as children. How similar they are to people today – human nature hardly
changes, if it does at all.

At least the military experience of Cleachus, who was about 50
years old, commanded the respect of his fellow officers and his stern
administration of discipline generated the fear as well as the respect
of the common soldiers, as Xenophon makes clear. By contrast, his
friend Proxenus, an intelligent and wealthy young Boetian aged
about 30 but lacking in military experience, was neither respected nor
feared by the soldiers. Xenophon gives us this pen-portrait of him:

> He was a good commander for people of a gentlemanly type, but he
> was not capable of impressing his soldiers with a feeling of respect or
> fear for him. Indeed, he showed more diffidence in front of his soldiers
> than his subordinates showed in front of him, and it was obvious that
> he was more afraid of being unpopular with his troops than his troops
> were afraid of disobeying his orders. He imagined that to be a good
> general, and to gain the name for being one, it was enough to give
> praise to those who did well and to withhold it from those who did
> badly. The result was that decent people in his entourage liked him, but
> unprincipled people undermined his position, since they thought he
> was easily managed.

Cleachus, at least, had the authority of *knowledge* and a commanding *presence*, yet he lacked a quality that Xenophon came to see as the very essence of leadership – *the ability to inspire willing obedience in others*.

What a true leader needs, said Xenophon, is a true knowledge of human nature. If he has that knowledge, then such a leader will be able to get the very best out of people. In the military context that will always give him the competitive edge over an enemy whose commanders lack that knowledge.

If leaders are *made* in the sense that they can acquire the authority of knowledge, are they *born* as far as the capacity to inspire the willing obedience of others is concerned? It is tempting to conclude that this is the case. The ability to give people the intellectual and moral strength to venture or persevere in the presence of danger, fear or difficulty is not the common endowment of all men and women. Xenophon, however, did believe that at least the basic principles of it could be acquired through education, as he had experienced himself with Socrates.

THE SOCRATIC TRADITION: CAN LEADERSHIP BE LEARNT?

In the narrow sense of the Situational Approach, anything that trains or equips a person with skill, technique, theoretical knowledge and practical application within a field is ipso facto training for leadership. Remember the proverb: 'Authority flows to the one who knows.' But it is unlikely that it will be seen by most people as such, for knowledge and technical knowledge are more like a necessary condition for leadership, rather than an essential strand of leadership itself.

The Socratic tradition, however, sows the seed that there is another kind of knowledge that a good leader should have. Can it be taught or is it innate? Xenophon, a religious man, hovers between a belief that this knowledge of inspiring others to work willingly and cheerfully is a divine gift, and a belief that it can be learnt. As I have implied, he must have felt that what he had learnt through the teaching of

Socrates had equipped him as a leader, probably in more ways than he would have been able to put his finger upon.

'Mind you, I do not go as far as to say that this can be learnt at sight or at a single hearing,' he wrote in the conclusion of *Oeconomicus*, his treatise on estate management! 'On the contrary, to acquire these powers a man needs education.' Natural potential is most important, he continues. But in some men leadership amounts to a gift, something akin to genius, which suggests something more of divine origin than human. This 'power to win willing obedience' may seem ultimately as if it is a gift of the gods, writes Xenophon, but it is not capriciously bestowed. The true beneficiaries of it are 'those who devote themselves to seeking wisdom'. There speaks the voice of Socrates!

By theorizing that there is a common or general element that transcends all the particular *fields* of human enterprise, Xenophon begins to take us away from the narrowest 'horses for courses' version of the Situational Approach. For he indicates, without specifying, a wider knowledge that a good leader needs, which is not the same as technical or professional skill, knowledge and experience. It is the knowledge of people, a knowledge of how to work with the grain of human nature as opposed to running up against it.

Field Marshal Lord Slim, the World War II general who more than the others of all nations reflected most deeply about leadership, was equally clear on that point. Primarily with the military field in mind (though he had worked in the steel industry before becoming a soldier), this is what he had to say on the subject in an address on 'Leadership in Management', given in 1957 in Australia where he was Governor-General:

> I said [the leader] must have knowledge. A man has no right to set himself up as a leader – or to be set up as a leader – unless he knows more than those he is to lead. In a small unit, a platoon say – or maybe a workshop gang – the leader should be able to do the job of any man in the outfit better than he can. That is a standard that should be required from all junior leaders.
>
> As the leader rises higher in the scale, he can no longer, of course, be expected to show such mastery of the detail of all the activities under him. A Divisional Commander need not know how to coax a wireless

set, drive a tank, preach a sermon or take out an appendix as well as the people in his division who are trained to do those things. But he has got to know how long these jobs should take, what their difficulties are, what they need in training and equipment and the strain they entail.

As the leader moves towards the top of the ladder, he must be able to judge between experts and technicians, and to use their advice although he will not need their knowledge. One kind of knowledge that he must always keep in his own hands – is that of men.

You can see that Slim – who told me when I asked him that he had not read Xenophon – is singing from the same hymn sheet. Knowledge of one's professional *field* is vital, but not the ability to do every technical or specialist job. Knowledge of people – human nature – is equally important. How does one acquire that?

Thus the Situational Approach completes the picture. It is the third path on the mountain. It also converges with the other two as it approaches the summit of the mountain. To change the metaphor from mountain paths to chemistry, the three elements – Qualities, Group and Situational – at first were like a chemical mixture; they could be separated by physical means, like sand or water. Now they have become a compound, to all intents a whole. Only for the purposes of teaching can we separate by chemical means that compound into its original components.

Leader and *leadership* are abstract terms. To repeat the point, you never see a *leader*, just as you never eat *fruit* – only apples or grapes. Cleachus, Proxemus and Xenophon are 'apples' – soldiers who are also leaders. Leadership is always embodied. Xenophon's Greek mind, inspired by Socrates, sought to discover the universal laws that explain why, given that human nature is common, some leaders inspire willing obedience while other commanders or managers fail to do so.

Centuries later a famous diplomat, one who would lose his life in a plane crash on a peace mission to Africa, asked himself the same questions. Dag Hammarskjöld, then Secretary-General of the United Nations, kept a journal, later published under the title of *Markings* (Faber, 1964). One night he wrote an entry in it on the theme of humility and the effect it has on others. He addressed his words to himself but they are relevant to you and me:

> Your position never gives you the right to command. It only imposes on you the duty of so living your life that others may receive your orders without being humiliated.

5

Levels of Leadership

The summits of the various kinds of business are, like the tops of mountains, much more alike than the parts below – the bare principles are much the same; it is only the rich variegated details of the lower strata that so contrast with one another. But it needs travelling to know that the summits are the same. Those who live on one mountain believe that their mountain is wholly unlike all others.

Walter Bagehot

Leadership exists on different levels. Thinking of organizations, there are three broad levels or domains of leadership:

- *Team*   The leader of a team of some 10 to 20 people with clearly specified tasks to achieve.
- *Operational*   The leader of one of the main parts of the organization and more than one team leader are under one's control. It is already a case of being a leader of leaders.
- *Strategic*   The leader of a whole organization, with a number of operational leaders under one's personal direction.

A chemical company employs 588 people. The managing director has seven people reporting to her, and each of those has seven responsible to them. At the lowest level there are 12 people in each work group. That means only *three* levels of leadership, as shown in Figure 5.1.

This is the simplest form of organization. If you look at the Rule of St Benedict, for example, you will see clearly the three levels of leadership in the large monasteries the Rule envisages. As organizations

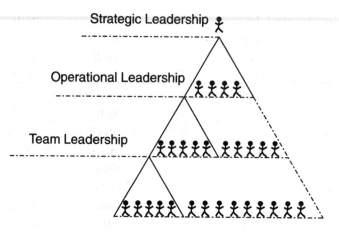

Figure 5.1   The three levels of leadership

get larger and more complex, more ranks, grades and levels come into the picture. But you should train your eye to discern the three key levels – they are always there.

A simple recipe for organizational success is to have effective leaders occupying these roles and working together in harmony as a team. That is simple enough to say: I am not implying that it is easy either to achieve or to maintain that state of affairs under the pressures of life today. But what is your alternative?

Within each broad level there may be subdivisions. The levels also overlap considerably. But the distinction is still worth making.

Sometimes, however, these three floor levels of the organizational house are disguised by the elaborate façade of hierarchy. A *hierarchy* (from Greek *hierus*, sacred) originally meant a ruling body of priests or clergy organized into orders or ranks each subordinate to the one above. The Greek *archos* was a generic term for a person who was in authority over others, their leader. It comes from a verb that means both to begin and to take the lead. Hence our English suffix *-archy* and prefix *arch-*, which means government or leadership of or by an *arch*. An *archbishop*, for example, is the first or leader among bishops, whereas *monarchy* is rule by one person – a king or emperor.

In Greek phalanxes and Roman formations there were *archoi* of various names among the rank-and-file. But once battle was joined, formations tended to disintegrate and the natural 'leaders of 10' emerged to rally and lead their comrades forward.

The foundation is the team leader, a truth that continues to evade many large organizations today. 'Ten soldiers wisely led will beat one hundred without a head,' wrote the Greek poet Euripides, as you may recall. A *decanus* in Greek and Latin was the leader of 10 soldiers. From its use in monastic orders for a monk in charge of ten others, the word comes down to us in the form of dean – the dean of a cathedral or the dean of a university faculty. Our military equivalent is corporal, which derives, like captain, from Latin *caput*, head. *Chief*, coming from *chef*, the French for a head, has the same meaning. Because as humans we stand erect, we tend to assume that a head is a hierarchical model: the head is on top so it is important. But look at any other animal: the head always goes *first* – it is the body's leader.

THE APPLICATION OF THE THREE CIRCLES TO ORGANIZATIONS

It was an Indian professor of management at a conference in Penang, Malaysia, who first pointed out to me that if the Three Circles model did not apply to organizations it was not a complete theory.

> Truth is not satisfied until… we are not impelled to strive for another and a better way of holding it all together. Truth is not satisfied, in other words, until it is all-containing and one.
>
> (A N Whitehead, *Essays on Truth and Reality*, 1914)

To be, in Whitehead's words, 'all-containing and one', the theory behind Functional Leadership had to link the microcosm of the small working group and the macrocosm of the working organization. In fact there was no satisfactory general theory of organization, merely lots of more or less incoherent writings on the subject. Could the Three Circle model do its magic at organizational level?

So in *Effective Leadership* (Pan, 1983) I began to explore the organizational possibilities of the Three Circles model. The basic philosophy, you recall, would suggest, at this level, that all *organizations* are unique (group personality, culture, ethos), but all share in common the three

STRATEGIC LEADERSHIP

ROLE | FUNCTIONS

- Providing direction for the organization as a whole.
- Getting strategy and policy right.
- Making it happen (overall executive responsibility).
- Organizing or reorganizing (balance of whole and parts).
- Releasing the corporate spirit.
- Relating the organization to other organizations and society as a whole.
- Choosing today's leaders and developing tomorrow's leaders.

Figure 5.2 The seven functions of a strategic leader

areas of interactive need: task, team and individual. What changes, of course, are the substantives (but not the nature) of the three terms.

THE ROLE OF THE STRATEGIC LEADER

The next step was a surprisingly easy one. If the Three Circles model – the Group or Functional Approach – applied to organizations as well as groups, then the model gave us the generic role of a strategic leader. It could be represented as in Figure 5.2.

Incidentally, as far as I know I was the first person to introduce the phrase *strategic leadership* in the early 1970s. Subsequently I discovered that in that phrase the word *leadership* is actually redundant. For in Greek *strategy* is made up of two words: *stratas*, a large body of people, and the *egy* element which means leadership. Strategy is simply the art of leading an organization.

Another way of understanding the functions that compromise the role of a strategic leader is to see them as covering the following key areas of the organization's forwards-moving, dynamic life:

- purpose/vision;
- strategic thinking and planning;
- operational/administration;

■ organization fitness to situational requirement;
■ energy, morale, confidence, esprit de corps;
■ allies and partners, stakeholders, political;
■ teaching and leading the learning by example.

What fits a person to fulfil this role? It is clearly a demanding and challenging one, even though there are professional staff at hand – sometimes in cohorts to help the strategic leader where the responsibilities are great.

Let us assume that the strategic leader has awareness, understanding and skill in the Three Circles model. Assume, too, that he or she knows their business. Take for granted as well personal leadership qualities such as enthusiasm, integrity, fairness, toughness, calmness, humanity and resilience.

IS IT POSSIBLE TO TRANSFER AS A STRATEGIC LEADER FROM ONE ORGANIZATION TO ANOTHER?

In theory or principle, strategic leaders are more transferable from one field of human enterprise to another, because they do not need the kind of specialized technical or professional knowledge that is required at the lower levels (the Situational Approach). As Walter Bagehot, in words quoted at the head of this chapter astutely observed, 'the summits of the various kinds of business… are the same', even though inhabitants of organizations always believe they are *totally* unique.

The idea that leadership is transferable – at a certain level – from one field to another can be found in tradition – another example of how the general philosophy of this book recovers, relates and progresses all the important strands of human thought on the subject. In the following dialogue we see more of Xenophon's mind at work than Socrates, his original inspiration and mentor.

THE CASE OF ANTISTHENES: BUSINESS LEADER TURNED GENERAL

Once, on seeing Nicomachides returning from the elections, Socrates asked him, 'Who have been chosen generals, Nicomachides?'

'Isn't it just like the Athenians?' Nicomachides replied. 'They have not chosen me after all the hard work I have done since I was called up, in the command of company or regiment, though I have been so often wounded in action.' (Here he uncovered and showed his scars.) 'They have chosen Antisthenes, who has never served in a marching regiment nor distinguished himself in the cavalry and understands nothing but money-making.'

'Isn't that a recommendation,' said Socrates, 'supposing he proves capable of supplying the men's needs?'

'Why,' retorted Nicomachides, 'merchants also are capable of making money, but that doesn't make them fit to command an army!'

'But,' replied Socrates, 'Antisthenes also is eager for victory, and that is a good point in a general. Whenever he has been choir-master, you know, his choir has always won.'

'No doubt,' conceded Nicomachides, 'but there is no analogy between the handling of a choir and of an army.'

'But you see,' said Socrates, 'though Antisthenes knows nothing about music or choir training, he showed himself capable of finding the best experts in these activities. And therefore if he finds out and prefers the best men in warfare as in choir training, it is likely that he will be victorious in that too; and probably he will be more ready to spend money on winning a battle with the whole state than on winning a choral competition with his tribe.'

'Do you mean to say, Socrates, that the man who succeeds with a chorus will also succeed with an army?'

'I mean that, whatever a man controls, if he knows what he wants and can get it he will be a good controller, whether he controls a chorus, an estate, a city or an army.'

'Really, Socrates,' cried Nicomachides, 'I should never have thought to hear you say that a good businessman would make a good general!'

By his familiar method of patient cross-examination, Socrates won agreement from Nicomachides that successful businessmen and generals perform much the same functions. Then Socrates proceeded to identify six of these functions or skills:

■ selecting the right man for the right job;
■ punishing the bad and rewarding the good;

■ winning the goodwill of those under them;
■ attracting allies and helpers;
■ keeping what they have gained;
■ being strenuous and industrious in their own work.

'All these are common to both,' Nicomachides accepted, 'but fighting is not.'

'But surely both are bound to find enemies?'

'Oh yes, they are.'

'Then is it not important for both to get the better of them?'

'Undoubtedly; but you don't say how business capacity will help when it comes to fighting.'

'That is just where it will be most helpful,' Socrates concluded. 'For the good businessman, through his knowledge that nothing profits or pays like a victory in the field, and nothing is so utterly unprofitable and entails such heavy loss as a defeat, will be eager to seek and avoid what leads to defeat, will be prompt to engage the enemy if he sees he is strong enough to win, and, above all, will avoid an engagement when he is not ready.'

For the most part, I have argued, this discussion is now only a theoretical or academic one. That is because I am a disciple of Socrates in believing that field-related knowledge and experience are essential strands in leadership. True, someone of above-average intelligence, that is, someone who learns quickly, can acquire knowledge of a new field, but experience takes much longer. In times past transfers from being a civilian to becoming a military commander were not uncommon. Oliver Cromwell, for example, was over 40 when he became a soldier and first commanded a troop of cavalry; within a year or two he was a famous general. T E Lawrence was under 30 years and had no military experience when he became in effect a strategic military leader. Reading Xenophon, as I mentioned earlier, helped to prepare him for the challenge.

Moving in the other direction, the Labour Government in 1946 chose General Sir William Slim, the celebrated commander-in-chief of the Fourteenth Army, to be Chairman of British Rail, for Attlee's Cabinet was convinced that industry needed the kind of leadership at the top which Slim had showed in Burma. Where else could they get it but from the Army? Slim was well into his apprenticeship as Vice-Chairman when he was whisked away to be Governor-General of Australia.

ON PRACTICAL WISDOM

As one reaches the top of an organization one has to deal with a greater level of complexity than at team or operational level. Complexity is both intellectually demanding and stressful, and it is not uncommon to discover that some individuals promoted to be chief executives just cannot handle it: they have risen to the level of their incompetence. In particular, they may lack the kind of mind that an effective strategic leader needs.

From ancient Athens I have borrowed the Greek word *phronesis* to describe the mind needed. As Aristotle discussed *phronesis* in the context of ethics, it is only really known today among moral philosophers. Translated into English as 'prudence' via the Latin *prudentia*, it has been robbed of significance, as 'prudence' now has the wrong overtones in English. The truest rendering of *phronesis* in English is by the phrase 'practical wisdom'. It is a particularly apt phrase because the Greeks saw *phronesis* as the key attribute of their best leaders, such as Pericles and Themistocles. Yet in English it is almost capable of being simplified into one word: 'wisdom', which derives from an old Anglo-Saxon word *wisian* meaning to show the way, to guide, to lead – wisdom is the thinking appropriate to a leader.

So *practical wisdom*, as opposed to *sophia* – the wisdom sought by the old philosophers – is the wisdom of leaders relating to practice: what way to go, what to do next, when to do it, how to do it and with whom to do it. These are questions and issues that cannot be solved like mathematical problems or puzzles: they call for the exercise of *judgement*. What equips a person with good judgement?

I suggest that wisdom is a compound of three elements: *intelligence*, *experience* and *goodness*. The inclusion of the latter may cause surprise, but you may notice that we never call bad people wise.

We are only on the threshold of the study of *phronesis*, practical wisdom, in the context of leadership, and so I cannot tell you much more about it. *Integrity* is simply one aspect of goodness. *Humility* makes an early entrance on the stage, as does *humour* and – more surprisingly – a certain *lightness of touch.*

The common idea is that we tend to grow wiser as we grow older. There is a counter-view, however, that the young are wise and that we lose wisdom as we get older – no fool like an old fool. Solomon was a byword for being wise as a young king, but where was wisdom in his later years?

Wisdom is a broad term, then, and suggests a rare combination of discretion, maturity, keenness of intellect, broad experience, extensive learning, profound thought and compassionate understanding. In its fullest application, wisdom implies the highest and noblest exercise of the moral nature as well as of the nature.

Yet wisdom always tends towards simplicity. It has no need of regular shaving with Occam's Razor, because it is always simplifying, always mentally spring cleaning, always reducing things to essentials. As Lao Tzu said:

> *In pursuit of knowledge, every day something is acquired;*
> *In pursuit of wisdom, every day something is dropped.*

PART 2

How to Grow Leaders –
The Seven Principles

By the end of Part 2 you will have grasped the seven principles that need to be applied if leadership is to be grown. It is not easy to distribute these principles between the individual concerned (the person who wishes to grow as a leader) and the organization that he or she happens to be working for at the time. The best results spring from a kind of partnership or informal contract between the two.

Principles are not rules or logical steps in a plan. There is no formula. Principles are general statements that are universally or widely considered to be true and fundamental. In Part 2, then, you have the opportunity to reflect upon the elementary propositions that have to guide or govern *any* effective organizational or personal programme for growing leaders, even if your client is only yourself. The principles – in no order of importance – are like bricks that you have to build into a wall of your own design.

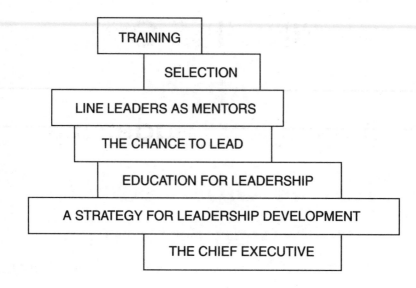

The seven principles of leadership development

PRINCIPLE ONE

Training for Leadership

There is nobody who cannot vastly improve his powers of leadership by a little thought and practice.

Lord Slim

Where does the story begin? Usually someone at or near the top of an organization – such as the chief executive, director of human resources or a senior divisional director – gets it into their heads that *leadership is a good thing and we should have more of it here*. Today there are plenty of outside pressures – not least in the public sector – to *do something about leadership* as well. There it comes from the politicians and their top advisers, who at last have come to see that reforms and 'modernization' of the public services depend upon effective *leadership*. Hence between 1999 and 2004 the UK government spend over £300 million in setting up *leadership* centres, colleges, foundations and councils. Why is all that effort proving to be so ineffective?

THE MOST COMMON ERROR

To act is easy, to think hard. This English proverb signposts the most common error: organizations act – for external or internal political reasons – before sitting down to think first. Managers are often pragmatic doers by nature, and any suggestion of a delay in order to think smacks of the Danish disease – so named by me after Hamlet, Prince of Denmark, who gave this classic description of it:

> Thus the native hue of resolution
> Is sicklied o'er with the pale cast of thought,
> And enterprises of great pith and moment,
> With this regard their currents turn awry,
> And lose the name of action.

The antidote to the Danish disease comes from an outstanding business leader of our times, the Canadian media magnate Roy Thomson, who once owned *The Times*. Writing in *After I Was Sixty* (Hamish Hamilton, 1975), he wrote:

> IBM – one of the world's great business organizations – have had for many years a single word as their motto. A sign over every executive's desk spells it out: Think. Let us be honest with ourselves and consider how averse we all are to doing just that. Thinking is work. In the early stages of a man's career it is very hard work. When a difficult decision or problem arises, how easy it is, after looking at it superficially, to give up thinking about it. It is easy to put it from one's mind. It is easy to decide that it is insoluble or that something will turn up to help us. Sloppy and inconclusive thinking becomes a habit. The more one does it the more one is unfitted to think a problem through to a proper conclusion.
>
> If I have any advice to pass on, as a successful man, it is this: if one wants to be successful, one must think; one must think until it really hurts. One must worry a problem in one's mind until it seems there cannot be another aspect of it that hasn't been considered. Believe me, that is hard work and, from my close observation, I can say that there are few people who are prepared to perform this arduous and tiring work.

I hope that you and your organization don't fall into that last category. To grow leaders and leadership does demand clear thinking. But I trust, too, that I shall show in this book that clear thinking about leadership is not really hard work – it is fun.

Organizations that rush or slide into 'leadership' activities without doing the necessary hard thinking exhibit the following symptoms:

- There is no clear concept of what leadership is and how it relates to management.
- There is no understanding of the different levels of leadership and their different training/educational requirements.
- Commitment (and sometimes even interest) is lacking at the very top.
- Ignorance about the history of thinking about leadership and the history of leadership training is prevalent – programmes often reflect the latest US fad or fashion.
- What is looked for is a 'quick fix' – instant leadership – and when it isn't forthcoming such organizations move on to the next panacea.

Organizations that want to avoid the most common error, however, are faced with a problem. The object of thinking is the truth. But to think out the truth about leadership or leadership development from – as we say – first principles, would take forever. Einstein once said: 'I think and think, for months, for years. Ninety-nine times the conclusion is wrong. The hundredth time I am right.' Still, as a result, now you and I don't have to puzzle out the Special Theory of Relativity for ourselves. Nor do designers of aircraft have to work out for themselves the Laws of Aerodynamics. There *is* a clear path of thought on leadership, but an organization cannot just take it from the expert: it needs to retrace that path and make it its own – hence Part 1 of this book.

What happens is that organizations don't think. They don't ask the right questions and weigh the possible solutions or courses of action. 'Thinking begins', wrote John Dewey, 'in what may fairly enough be called a forked-road situation, a situation that is ambiguous, that presents a dilemma, that proposes alternatives.'

If an organization doesn't think for itself then it becomes especially vulnerable to people who offer to do its thinking for it – at a price. But this doesn't really solve the problem. Besieged by management consultants, business schools, gurus and books that are all selling 'answers' on leadership or leadership development, how does one know which guide to follow?

To make matters worse, these self-nominated guides are blind themselves. For the academics, consultants and teachers of leadership have not *thought* about leadership in the sense that Einstein thought about physics or Frederick Lanchester about aerodynamics. Therefore they are as confused and as muddled as their clients. And, as the proverb says, 'If the blind lead the blind, both will fall into the pit.'

Consequently, it isn't easy for an organization today to think for itself about leadership and leadership development – the waters are so muddied. Not easy but by no means impossible. ICI did it in the 1980s, thus breaking a sound barrier in this field. Because virtually no other organization since then has followed suit is not an argument for saying that it is impossible. Far from it. All you need to do is to get your strategic leadership team together for 24 hours and think about the questions that this book addresses.

CASE STUDY: ICI IN 1983

We must obey the greatest law of change. It is the most powerful law of nature. Edmund Burke

In September 1981 Bill Stead and Edgar Vincent – the two senior managers responsible for group human resources in ICI – came to see me at the University of Surrey. They gave me some background about the plight of ICI – 1980 had been a disastrous year in which profits fell by 48 per cent and the dividend was cut for the first time since formation in 1926 – and told me that the executive directors had decided that the first priority in human resources strategy should be the development of what they called manager-leaders. They wished me to act as outside consultant.

My previous contacts with ICI had been few and far between. In the 1970s I knew it from afar as a company that had spent hundreds of thousands of pounds on hiring behavioural scientists, mainly American and some most distinguished, such as Douglas McGregor. Some innovations, for example the work on job enrichment, had had a high profile. It had a reputation for sophistication in its various management systems and management development programmes. Through the agency of the Chemical and Allied Products Industrial Training Board in the 1970s I spent a few days at ICI's ammonia plant on Teesside as co-trainer on a course for supervisors. That was about the sum of my knowledge.

Edgar Vincent asked me if I could suggest other organizations that had used my ideas to grow leaders, except the Army, which he and his colleague had already visited. I remember being stuck for an answer. There were of course many organizations – some 2,000 of them in 1981 – that were sending managers and supervisors on action-centred leadership (ACL) courses, or even putting the whole management through an ACL programme but that was not the question put to me. I could think of no organizations that were *growing* leaders in the ways I had been recommending. I suggested that ICI might like to be the first real guinea pig, and the pair of them thought that would be an excellent idea. They also suggested that in exchange such a project should prove an extremely valuable opportunity within the context of my own research into leadership and leadership development.

After some further discussions with Edgar, now Group Human Resources Manager, we agreed upon a plan to get the ball rolling. Instead of my writing a paper on strategy or the board issuing a set of edicts, it was decided that a major conference would be convened at Warren House, ICI's conference centre, at which a cross-section of able top managers in ICI's nine divisions could meet and discuss the matter, hearing from various specialists like me in the course of three days. Then it would be left up to them to identify the right strategy for ICI, and for their own divisions within it, in order to achieve the first of ICI's key HR policies – the development of management-leaders.

The Warren House conference

The Warren House conference took place in January 1982, based upon a programme that Edgar and I had worked out together. As consultant I was present throughout. I also gave one talk about the functional approach to leadership, together with some reminders about the contribution of Maslow and Herzberg, and the importance of understanding the decision-making continuum. Apart from the human resources director and chairman of ICI, the other speakers were Peter Prior (chairman of Bulmers), David Gilbert-Smith (Leadership Trust), and Andrew Stewart (a psychologist and independent management consultant who spoke about methods of selecting or assessing leaders).

Since my initial meeting with Edgar and his colleague, ICI had appointed in November a new chairman from among its three deputy chairmen – not the one that had been mentioned to me as the most likely. Edgar evidently regarded his appointment as a considerable bonus to the enterprise of leadership development that we were engaged upon. I met John Harvey-Jones for the first time in the bar at Warren House that evening (27 January) and he spoke to the conference informally after supper.

The chairman began by saying that ICI was wrongly positioned in the real growth markets of the Far East and the USA. This picture had implications for management style/leadership pattern. 'We have first class management,' he said, 'but it has become excessively bureaucratic and political. We've adopted a value system that is ponderous, negative, unanxious to share risk and not willing to give headroom.

'What's the pattern for the next 10 years? Instability and change will characterize it. It will be a repositioning decade, with lots of new patterns and shifts of power. Growth, as we've known it, will be greatly reduced. No company can exist without growth, therefore we have to make it by pinching the markets of competitors, outdating his products and developing new ones,' John Harvey-Jones continued. He talked some more about how he saw the emergence of some giants in the chemical industry in Europe, a pattern like the one in the USA. Technologically we were in for enormous change.

'What do we need to work in this environment?' he next asked. 'A new attitude to risk – we minimize risk, we don't maximize opportunities. But the biggest risk of all is to take no risk. We have to be flexible, because we won't read the future right. We need to have an ability to move fast, more market sensitivity, more openness and trust, greater tolerance of differences and more courage in dealings with others. Individuals have the answers, not ICI as a group.'

John Harvey-Jones then turned to his work plans after he became formally chairman in April. He would start at the top with the board. 'Let's meet in the middle. We haven't got time for a slow trickle-down.' 'Double-guessing would be cut out by having fewer people – the size of the board would be reduced for a start.' The discussion that followed was exceptionally frank on all sides. In response to one question the chairman pointed to 'the catalytic things we can do' to encourage entrepreneurial enterprise. 'The present ICI system will kill any business! The dynamic has been increasingly centralized. One of my jobs at every level has been to hold an umbrella over my chaps' heads. Senior management is about getting people to own the problem and to do something about it, not passing it up. Our system must be not to have a system.'

A sense of urgency coloured his closing remarks. It is a race against time – we are too late – the world is breaking up – bits to be grabbed now. His vision of an adaptable, open, flexible, fast-moving ICI – ready to move quickly in perceived thrusts or direc-tions. 'We've got to grow this new ICI.' Asked about the attitude of his fellow directors he said that he couldn't order them. 'I have to lead the board to lead. They voted for me. There is no such thing as one leader. What matters most is a common sense of val-ues. Leadership is about getting extraordinary performance out of ordinary people. In ICI we have got extraordinary people to begin with.'

In answer to another question John Harvey-Jones highlighted another strength. 'ICI exists through its ability to work informal systems. We have got the ability to work together informally. I'm keen on clarity of organizational responsibilities, but we've got to keep this informal ability to work together, because we'll never get the structure right. We start miles ahead of any other European chemical company; we have shown in the last two years that we can be unbelievably fast. We've got a lot going for us, such as a good technological basis. In other respects I could wish we were better placed. But we can knock the hell out of the opposition.'

Inspired by those words and determined to end the 'treacle', as they called it, which the ICI bureaucratic culture had created, the participants in the conference continued working all next day on their strategic plans for liberating the leadership and enterprise within ICI.

Leadership training in ICI

Among the recommendations each of the nine divisional teams resolved to introduce leadership training based upon the Three Circles approach – task, team and individual – which I had outlined. In keeping with the new emphasis on decentralization, it was left to the divisions to devise their own leadership training programmes, using me as a resource. My contribution varied accordingly. Looking through my diaries I see that I spoke to all the senior managers in one division; spent three days at Warren House with all the finance directors and their teams; advised one division on its leadership course and did some on-the-spot 'training of the trainers' after the first one; did some counselling sessions with some divisional directors on an individual basis; advised four managers who had been asked to make recommendations on the key issue of leadership to the board of the Organics Division; reviewed ICI's methods of selecting graduates; and carried out an evaluation survey of all the external leadership courses currently being used by ICI. But perhaps my most important contribution was to lead a one-day seminar each year for four years with Edgar Vincent for the nine divisional training managers responsible for the functional leadership courses in their various forms.

It is not within my compass here to say more about the radical changes that have taken place during the chairmanship of Sir John Harvey-Jones, which ended in 1987, especially as Sir John himself is writing a book on the subject. As I mentioned earlier, in 1984 ICI was the first British company to break the one billion pound profit barrier (the second, National Westminster Bank, has also made continual use of ACL since its introduction in 1969).

Of course the success of ICI in the period under review cannot be ascribed entirely to leadership, although I don't suppose that anyone would deny the importance of leadership as shown by Sir John Harvey-Jones and by many other ICI manager-leaders at every level in the divisions. As for leadership development, all that can be safely said is that it has proved to be not incompatible with business success.

Leadership is about getting extraordinary performance out of ordinary people. Sir John Harvey-Jones

Key outcomes

■ In 1981 the board of ICI accepted a key human resources strategy as part of its overall business strategy of repositioning and regenerating ICI. (The HR director is one of the seven or eight directors on the main board.) That overall strategy has been successful: ICI is back among the world leaders in the chemical and pharmaceutical industries. 'Just as we need a business vision for the future we need a people vision too,' said Harvey-Jones in 1982 to the representatives of ICI's employees. A good selection procedure has ensured that ICI had a good supply of actual and potential manager-leaders.

■ The main thrust of the new programmes in leadership training for managers and supervisors came within the nine divisions. All these programmes used the Three Circles model as the basis of their teaching about good leadership in management.

■ Like all large companies ICI had faced the problem that divisions tended not to release people for career development purposes. However, it made substantial progress in that direction.

■ The importance is stressed of managers knowing their people as individuals, dealing with them face-to-face and getting their support.

■ A small 'research and advisory' team – the Group HR Manager and his divisional counterparts – guided the leadership training programme.

■ Layers of hierarchy and scores of committees were scythed away in the division and at headquarters, where Harvey-Jones dispensed with two deputy chairmen and reduced the size of the main board. One divisional board was reduced from 20 directors to six. A rigorous policy of decentralizing decision-making authority and central services, such as purchasing and shipping, was followed.

■ Much more emphasis was put on individuals using their own initiative and 'owning' their own self-development.

■ In the 1970s ICI suffered from the problems of size. According to a senior ICI man 'it employed too many high paid people to check and crosscheck other men's figures. It was an over-educated company. It had a technical bias, was not breeding people with entrepreneurial flair.' A new organizational climate has begun to emerge in which leadership can grow and flourish. The chairman's role was strengthened into that of chief executive (called 'principal executive officer' in ICI). As tenant of it, Sir John Harvey-Jones not only showed leadership by giving the company a sense of direction – 'I hope I am a leader but I'm not a one-man band' – but did all in his power to encourage it in others. He talked about it, placing it high in his list of values. He took part in training courses, and in one year met more than 8,000 ICI managers in group discussions.

How do you know you have won? When the energy is coming the other way and when your people are visibly growing individually and as a group.

Sir John Harvey-Jones

THE SECOND MOST COMMON ERROR

Organizations that don't think hard adopt the unconscious assumption that leadership development is something *that starts and stops with senior management.* They spend immense amounts of money on in-house leadership programmes, sending people on 'designer label' programmes at prestigious business schools – preferably in the USA – and on providing their top managers with expensive one-on-one mentoring schemes, all in the name of leadership.

This unconscious strategy reflects the Zaleznik Error, the making of a false dichotomy between 'leaders' and 'managers'. A consequence was that some organizations concluded that they needed both 'leaders' – heroic or charismatic figures – *and* plodding 'managers'. So they bet their entire training budget on trying to turn their senior management into 'transformational leaders' – and predictably lost their money.

This unconscious assumption is also a curious survivor of the British class system. Management, like society, was divided into upper, middle and lower classes: executive directors and other senior executives with director or near-director status, middle managers, and supervisors and foremen (collectively renamed 'first-line managers'). Leadership was the preserve of the first group. Get that right and all else would follow.

This was always outdated thinking. Wise organizations always saw themselves as a hierarchy of three leadership levels: team, operational and strategic. One level is not superior to another in *importance* – there is no class system. They are different in levels of responsibility but equal in value. Therefore in principle there is no reason why more money should be spent on one level than upon another. Money should flow to the point where it can be used most effectively.

Where that point – or points – is in any given organization is a matter of judgement. But, as a general principle, it is more likely to be nearer the *team leadership* end of the spectrum. The reason is that younger people are far more likely to take on board both the generic role of leader and the attributes that naturally associate with it. By 'take on board' I mean learn. Of course we all go on learning throughout our lives, but there are 'windows of opportunity'. For example, if a child (for some very rare and extraordinary reason) misses the window for acquiring a language, it is virtually impossible for him or her to learn to communicate verbally in later life.

The natural starting point — team leaders

The basic principle in leadership development is that *an organization should never give a team leadership role or position to someone without training*. We don't entrust our children to bus drivers who are not trained; why place any kind of worker under leaders who have no training?

Before the pioneering work at Sandhurst that I described in Part 1 there was a reason for doing just that – it was not possible to train leaders. You could train managers or supervisors to manage or supervise, but *leadership* remained in the lap of the gods to bestow upon the favoured few. We now know that is not the case. You can train team leaders.

The way, as I have suggested, is not to attempt to teach them the attributes of leadership as if by frontal assault, but to go to the heart of the matter and teach the *generic role of a team leader*, using inevitably the Three Circles model because that *is* the generic role. You then establish an armature on which participants can build. Let *them* think for themselves how the role is shaped, applied or exercised in their given context – thus what specific actions they need to take.

The second reason for starting at this level is that team leadership is the principal seedbed for the organization's operational leaders, and they in turn are the seedbed for strategic leaders. So if you lay the right foundation at team leadership level you reap the rewards at the higher levels.

You can see this principle most clearly at work in the Services, for they do not (because they cannot) recruit incomers for operational/ strategic leadership roles. As they have been following the Adair philosophy in this respect for over a generation, you should expect to find that any general, admiral or air marshal would know the Three Circles as a matter of course. His education as a leader began – though it certainly did not finish – there.

Nowadays I am frequently asked to teach leadership at what are in effect operational and strategic levels, and I do so with great pleasure. But due to the present lack of any robust team leadership training outside the Services it is often like trying to teach English literature to those who haven't first mastered English grammar – basic sentence construction, punctuation, spelling, style, etc.

A third reason why an organization should look first at the team leadership level – and not last or not at all, as is the present case – is that it has most control at that point. Putting it bluntly, it is easier to require all newly appointed team leaders to attend a course than it is to get all operational or strategic leaders to do so. The reasons (or excuses) the latter offer are varied and often valid. So the whole constituency tends not to take part, so most fish who need St Peter's fingerprints on their back are going to slip through the leadership net.

Then why not do it at school or university?

There is a certain logic to this question. You could argue that the generic Three Circles model is critical for all effective team-working as well as effective leadership – the difference between a leader and team member is not a kilometre but a centimetre. Why not teach it at school – in the Scouts, Guides or Cadet Corps or in the National Curriculum, as a life skill?

My experience has included a number of experiments of my own in this area. Setting aside all the pragmatic and political reasons why teaching leadership on a large scale doesn't and won't happen in the UK secondary education system, there is an underlying hypothesis that I hold which reconciles me to this state of affairs. It's back to the 'window of opportunity' thesis – there is a *too soon* as well as a *too late*. A certain age or maturity, a certain amount of experience in real work groups, and a certain trepidation at impending leadership responsibility: these are the bricks that form together the threshold of the 'window of opportunity'. Before they are there you are writing on water.

I hasten to add that this is a hypothesis. Given proper training methods and professionally trained teachers, it may be proved to be false. Moving it up to university or higher education level would remove one objection – the age or maturity level. Moreover, the prevalence of 'gap years' introduces some work experience. Again, I have carried out various experiments here, the most successful being at the University of Surrey where all engineering students since 1983 have gone through a leadership course based on the Three Circles, using the Functional Leadership/ACL model; it is now an integral part of becoming an engineer and has been brilliantly taught by a team of lecturers in the various engineering departments. I have also conducted experiments with more general groups at the University of York and Churchill College, Cambridge, both in association with the university career services.

If the 'window of opportunity' is age related – namely that we take on board the really big ideas of our lives when we are in the 'long' 18–22 years age bracket, it would be logical to do something then. After all, all organizations now look to graduates for their future leaders. Even the Services, which were once an alternative form of higher education to universities, have changed their tune: now 87 per cent of officers under training are graduates, compared to nil in the 1960s. Is it already *almost too late* at 23 or 24?

The honest answer is that we do not know. There are, of course, immense practical difficulties in actually teaching leadership at universities, though not quite impossible ones, as the Surrey example shows. But the bigger problem is that students for the most part lack a sense of relevance, they don't know the context. The world of work remains a distant prospect for those studying for a degree and enjoying life on a university campus. Work experience – a modern gateway to graduate employment – will take up any discretionary time in the career-oriented area. One could introduce a nationally recognized 'team leadership certificate' for students, which would undoubtedly be very attractive to employers of graduates, but in the UK we are 10 years away from doing anything like that, and even then it will probably only attract a small minority of customers.

My conclusion, then, is that in the foreseeable future your organization – or your field of enterprise – is going to own the problem of training team leaders and team members. The secondary or tertiary education system is, rightly or wrongly, not about to relieve you of this burden – or, I should say, opportunity.

TRAINING TEAM LEADERS

You should start by taking an inventory of what your organization is at present doing to train team leaders before or shortly after their first appointment. Here are the questions you should ask:

- How many team leaders does your organization employ?
- What is their average tenure of the role?

- Did they require or receive any extra professional or technical training?
- How are they equipped with any extra IT and financial/accountancy know-how?
- Do they undergo a leadership programme? If so:
  - How long is it?
  - What is the cost per head?
  - Do you do it yourself or outsource it?
  - Does it cover the generic role of leader?
  - Is it practical? Do people learn by doing?
- Have you read all (or a cross-section) of the final course evaluation sheets, together with action plans?
- Do your post-course evaluations – six months and 12 months later – support the thesis that the training is effective?
- What pre- and post-course e-learning material supports the initial team leadership course? How are team leaders reacting to it?

Given our expertise in this area now, we know that team leadership courses should be short – two days (or three at the most), conducted by a properly qualified trainer, and backed up by an e-learning capability. The hallmarks of such effective training are that it should be *simple, practical, relevant,* have *variety* (varied challenge-levels of exercises, case studies, films) and be a *dialogue,* not a monologue. If your course contains lectures or presentations lasting more than 10 minutes it is already on the wrong track.

In large organizations (for instance the NHS, which currently employs 386,400 nurses of whom 35,000 are in team leadership roles) you are looking for a team leadership course that is *high volume, high quality* and *low cost.*

In large organizations like the NHS, Armed Services, Police Services or Local Government, where the 'parts' of the whole enjoy considerable autonomy, including training, it is fatally easy for organizations to lose *the economies of size.* If everyone has to invent their own wheel, the wheels cost a lot of money – and wheels on one railway branch line then don't fit a track of different gauge, on another branch line. Nobody wants to see a soulless conformity in training, as everybody slavishly follows some head office prototype. But isn't it only common sense to pool resources, design and develop a master-course with plenty of options or variations? The sheer cost of developing excellent e-learning resources – something that has yet to be done in the leadership training field – dictates as much.

You can begin to see now why applying Principle Six, A Strategy for Leadership Development, starts to look attractive – especially if you happen to be Chancellor of the Exchequer. You can get so far by starting at the beginning and training your team leaders, and if you follow the recipe you will get good results. It really does work. But if you seek *excellence* you will soon begin to feel disquieted if the rest of the system is not playing its part to improve, support and build upon that initial breakthrough.

YOU DO NOT TEACH THE PATHS OF THE FOREST TO AN OLD GORILLA

Napoleon and Wellington were agreed on one thing: the greatest military leader of all time was Hannibal. When in exile in Asia Minor, seeking to elude the vengeance of the Rome he had so often humiliated in the field, Hannibal was persuaded reluctantly by his host to attend a seminar on 'military leadership' by a visiting academic. 'What did you think of it?' the king asked, as they left the room with the rest of the audience. Hannibal fixed him with his one remaining bright eye. 'In my time I have heard many old fools,' he said, 'but this one takes the prize.'

This is a cautionary tale against trying to instruct operational and strategic leaders in a subject in which they are better able to instruct you. The African proverb that is the heading of this section says as much. If you apply Principle Two, Selection – the subject of the next chapter – then the major parts of your organization will be led by those who already have the attribute of leadership. What do you intend to teach them?

The answer is, *not much*. All that such nominated operational leaders need before they take up their appointments is the opportunity to recalibrate; that is, to widen the diameter of their thinking about leadership and to relate it to the specific needs of this organization at this juncture of time. The same principles apply; the same generic role serves as a compass card. But the *task* is more complex, more multistranded and longer term; the *team* is much bigger, more diverse, probably more spatially separated and it may well include partners or allies who do not actually belong to the organization.

The individual is different, too. As Ovid wrote of one leader in *Heroides*: 'He is a leader of leaders.' To lead leaders you have to be really good, for leaders can be quite complex as individuals. There are comparatively few people in any field who can do it. The nearer you get to the top, the harder it is to find the right leader. 'An army of a thousand is easy to find; but, ah, how difficult to find a general' (Chinese proverb).

You will, of course, have detected that I have been outlining above something like an ideal situation – but, then, that's my job – to give you a vision. But I am aware, as T S Eliot wrote, that:

Between the idea and the reality...
Falls the Shadow.

What happens, in brief, is that organizations that don't grow leaders end up by having to fill slots with those who are poor leaders, if they are leaders at all. There is then an inevitable effect on morale.

But don't we need new gorillas?

In the UK context there is now plenty of available evidence to support the conclusion that organizations are short of good leaders. The Chartered Institute of Management's Leadership Project (2001) claimed to be a 'reality check' of leadership in UK organizations, based on a detailed survey of almost 1,500 practising managers in a broad cross-section of organizations and 30 personal interviews with 10 established leaders, 10 middle managers and 10 young people in the 18–24 years age group. The findings include:

■ Overall, the quality of leadership in UK organizations did not receive high ratings. Over a third of all managers, and almost half of junior managers, rate the quality of leadership in their organizations as poor. Public sector leadership received the lowest ratings.

■ Half (51 per cent) of all responding managers thought that their employers gave a low priority to leadership development, while 46 per cent said that there was no specific budget for training and developing potential leaders. Only 25 per cent said that there was a clear and articulated framework for leadership development.

■ The most senior managers and executives are far more likely than junior managers to rate the quality of leadership as high and to think that leadership development is an organizational priority.

■ Many of those interviewed thought leaders often *stop* learning at a particular point in their careers. Progression through senior positions does not always coincide with continuing professional development.

■ Responding managers rate the quality of leadership more highly if they are working in organizations that have a clear and systematic approach to leadership development.

Unfortunately, this survey only asked managers about how *they* were being led – not how they were leading. In other words, it reflected the Zaleznik Error that there are leaders at the top and managers in the middle. It was a kind of 360° appraisal – asking the 'managers' what they thought of their 'leaders'.

So, for example, 55 per cent of respondents identified *inspiration* as a characteristic that leaders should ideally possess, but only 11 per cent said that they had experienced it in reality. But they were not asked what *they* were doing to inspire others. Nobody thought of them as being leaders. The value of the report is further reduced by the bizarre – but all too typical – remark that 'successful leadership is defined by the goals of each organization or group of people, and not by a set of *a priori* truths.' It is precisely because organizations are not teaching 'a set of *a priori* truths' that they are in such trouble over leadership development. What is required, of course, is a form of leadership training which, to quote the respondents, 'emphasizes the links between theory and practice and helps individuals to put their learning in context'.

DO 'SHEEP DIPS' WORK?

The response of many organizations to the realization that their senior managers are in leadership positions *but are not leaders* has been to institute a one-off series of 'leadership programmes' or seminars which all managers have to go through. For example, I became a consultant to Exxon Chemicals in the United States in the 1980s, which put their 1,000 top managers worldwide through a leadership programme called 'Quest'. And I have also been involved personally in similar 'catch up' programmes in the former British Rail, in a merchant bank, and in two major clothes suppliers to Marks & Spencer. Such programmes are often dismissively referred to as 'sheep dips'.

Yet such programmes are better than nothing. As the proverb says, 'It is better to begin in the evening than not at all.' But their effect is limited. In my experience they are often like the seed in the biblical Parable of the Sower which, falling on shallow ground, shoots up in the early warmth of enthusiasm but lacks roots in the soil and eventually withers away. To change the metaphor, they are flash floods, generating torrents of enthusiasm but, without the turbines of the Three Circles being in place, they do not get turned into purposeful energy.

How often do organizations forget that there is no such thing as instant leadership? Growing leaders is like growing fruit trees. Other owners may one day have the benefit of your trees, but maybe you will also benefit from other unknown owners of orchards. The best organizations take pride in the fact that they grow more leaders than they need; they are net exporters of leaders.

How to grow leaders — a quick guide for orchard-owners

- Select good seed or stock   Choose people with natural potential for the generic role of leader.
   Look for the tell-tale signs that the spark of leadership is within them.
- Prepare the soil   Check out your corporate culture. Does it grow or stunt leadership growth?

Plough up your yesterday's paradigms and mindsets about management.

Are the fields the right size? Have you got the structure right?

■ Enrich the earth by fertilizing and watering Make sure the sun of good values – integrity, honesty, justice, fairness, etc has an unhindered path – cut out the jungle foliage that obscures the sun and the stars.

Invest in people – the better the people, the better the leaders will be.

■ Rotate the crops Give leaders a variety of challenges and opportunities.

■ Let the fields lie fallow Not all trees bear fruit every year. Even the best field needs to lie fallow. Give leaders time to think, to reflect and to catch up with themselves.

■ Observe where plants thrive A leader who struggles in one field or sector of it may be successful in another.

What is the leader's ecological niche? Where will he or she thrive?

■ Prune the dead wood Simplify, cut back to the trunk. Abandon the practices and ideas that don't work. Go back to basics.

■ Let the taproots go deep The water of inspiration lies deep underground. The trees that grow and bear fruit year by year have deep taproots.

The psychological contract

The agricultural analogy is limited, for we are not plants, trees or farm animals. But the points of comparison are that leaders grow naturally and growth takes time. What wise organizations do is to facilitate this growth as far as they can. Not for purely altruistic reasons: they need to keep the pick of the crop of leaders in order to change in positive and productive ways, to reach towards sustained success. It may be partly true that organizations grow leaders, but it is even more true to say that *leaders grow the business*.

My father worked for the same company, a family business, for over 40 years. He was loyal to the firm; the firm was loyal to him – during his army service in World War II, even when he was badly wounded by a bomb, his old job awaited him. As we all know now, that sort of psychological contract is a thing of the past. The new deal is that organizations will 'add value' to the employability of a manager, so that when he or she moves on their chances of making a step forwards is increased. It is a demanding responsibility, but effective leadership development is one key area where it can be done.

It would be an unwise graduate or other entrant of real potential and ambition who joined an organization that offered no training in team leadership. No wise organization that wanted to attract and retain the best of tomorrow's leaders would fail to establish (or access) a world-class team leadership training programme.

Putting it another way, if you meet the *individual* needs circle of the leader, which include personal growth, he or she will have a lot more to give to the *task* and the *team*.

HOW TO MANAGE LEADERSHIP TRAINING

Not all organizations by any means are large or wealthy enough to maintain their own training units or specialists. Directors of Human Resources tend to be generalists.

My own thinking is that in practice it is the chief executive who owns the problem of training team leaders as part of their inherent responsibility *as leaders* for growing tomorrow's leaders. They are the Head Gardener. But the executive or managerial part of it has to be delegated. To whom?

Again, at the risk of stating the obvious, there has to be someone in the organization who is responsible for leadership development (using it in the role sense, that phrase now encompasses management development). It is important to identify who that person is.

If you outsource your team leadership training to training specialists make sure you retain ownership of the content and the process of learning transfer – the action points. It has to reflect your practical philosophy – Principle Six again. The training company needs to be briefed on the whole strategy.

Partnerships (outsourcing is a partnership) call for leadership. Make sure you do the leading. Only sign a limited-term contract, and build in regular progress reviews.

Key points

■ A natural starting point for an organization that wants to grow leaders is *training*. Not middle or senior managers but team leaders. *The cardinal principle in leadership development is never to appoint someone a leader without the appropriate form of training or preparation.* Are you applying it?

■ Team leaders are at the base of a natural pyramid. They are the seedbed from which operational leaders come, and they in turn beget strategic leaders. The natural 'window of opportunity' for training leaders in the generic role/functions/qualities of leadership is when they are on the threshold of becoming team leaders at work for the first time. Miss that opportunity and you may have missed the boat.

■ The micro-principles and hallmarks of effective team leadership training are well established. With the exception of the Services, however, they are little understood and not practised. Therefore poor leadership is the normal condition in organizations.

■ Middle and senior managers who have had no good formal or informal leadership training when young seldom make up the deficiency. It is too late. Remedial programmes in the form of 'sheep dips' have only a very limited value, often not much more than salving the consciences of the HR department or as political tools to keep the government happy. They are seldom rigorously evaluated.

■ The chief error that most organizations – I mean here their top strategic leadership teams – make in this field is that they do not *think and think until it really hurts.* Lacking any clear thinking about leadership and how it relates to management, they are at the mercy of the winds.

■ Operational and strategic leaders who have been trained and tested at team leadership level do need further training/education-type experiences in leadership as part of their rites of passage: to review, to reflect, to recalibrate the Three Circles, to remind and to kindle again their torch of inspiration. Remember Seneca's words: 'Many might have attained to wisdom, had they not thought they had already attained it.'

There must be a beginning of any great matter, but the continuing unto the end until it be thoroughly finished yields the true glory.

Sir Francis Drake

PRINCIPLE TWO

Selection

Measure the cloth seven times, because it can only be cut once.
Russian proverb

This book is about growing leaders but it is actually very hard, maybe impossible, for an organization to grow leaders. Therefore – and here is a paradox for you – *choose people who are leaders already*.

But how do you know they are leaders or have the potential to be leaders? Is there any scientific way of assessing or judging leadership? In this chapter we shall explore these vitally important questions. The end result should be that your organization is able to better apply Principle Two – Selection.

HOW DO PEOPLE BECOME LEADERS?

How does anyone find themselves in the role of *leader*? There are four possible routes – not mutually exclusive:

- *Emergent.* The person concerned may simply emerge in a 'leaderless group' situation, as the perceived right person to lead the group. A form of election by informal acclamation.
- *Appointment.* In a hierarchy (all working organizations are hierarchical) a person may be appointed to a leadership role. This appointment is made by a superior or superiors to whom the leader remains accountable.

■ *Elected.* The group may be invited – or establish its right – to elect its own leader. In the political context this right is the essential principle of democracy. Here the leader is accountable to his or her electors.

■ *Hereditary.* A son or daughter may have as a birthright the legacy of leading an organization, community or nation. A *duke*, for instance, (from the Latin *dux*, leader) and *prince* (in Latin literally 'one who is taken as first') are medieval examples. Today family firm dynasties as well as remaining monarchies (as in Saudi Arabia) offer plenty of contemporary examples.

CHOOSING A NEW LEADER

Volunteers to man the new Penlee lifeboat, which will replace the one lost with all its crew a week ago, will start rigorous training this week. Twenty-five volunteers have come forward from the Cornish village of Mousehole where the dead crew members were based and will train under Leslie Visponds, of the RNLI.

In all, 16 people are believed to have died; eight crew members and the eight people aboard the coaster Union Star which the lifeboat was trying to rescue when it smashed into it. A government inquiry has begun into the disaster.

The man most likely to lead the new crew is Mike Sutherland, an experienced local seaman and Trinity House pilot; but the ultimate selection of the coxswain will depend on the training.

Visponds said yesterday: 'As the training proceeds, one man or maybe two will show that they have the right qualities and the right temperament to act as leader under the most difficult conditions, and the best crew members will also emerge.

'It is up to them to indicate who they would like to lead them, and I am hopeful that I shall be able to ratify their selection and choice.'

(Press Report, December 1981)

All these paths to leadership (role) in human society have their pros and cons. History, for example, has plenty to say about the downside of the *hereditary* method when it comes to nations. But kings and queens did have a potential advantage when leading armies in battle was a principal part of the job description of monarchy, for the hereditary principle could sweep a gifted leader to the top at a very young age. Alexander the Great is the classic example. Although not a king, Hannibal was lucky to inherit when still young the great army his father Hasdrubal had created. But leadership (attribute) is not genetic. Great fathers seldom have great sons. Randolph Churchill may have inherited some of his father's characteristics, but not those that made Winston Churchill the British nation's emergent leader in 1940.

The *emergent* situation is obviously the most natural one. Gandhi is the great example of a non-military leader, but he was never *appointed* or *elected* to political office in India. You usually need all three approaches – Qualities, Situational and Group or Functional – to explain why someone proves acceptable as a leader. A good test case is T E Lawrence, alias 'Lawrence of Arabia', who at the age of 28 emerged as a natural leader among the British military advisers to the Arab Revolt in World War I, many of them his senior in rank.

Colonel W F Stirling served with T E Lawrence in the desert, and recorded his impression of him as a leader in *T E Lawrence By His Friends* (ed A W Lawrence, Jonathan Cape, 1937), cited below.

CASE STUDY: T E LAWRENCE

Lawrence not only saw the task more clearly than others and how it could be achieved, but also possessed a remarkable intuitive sense of what was happening in the minds of the group. Above all, he led by example. It was my great good fortune to be appointed General Staff Officer to the Arab group. From then throughout the final phase of the Arab revolt on till the capture of Damascus, I worked, travelled, and fought alongside Lawrence. Night after night we lay wrapped in our blankets under the cold stars of the desert.

At these times one learns much of a man. Lawrence took the limelight from those of us professional soldiers who were fortunate enough to serve with him, but never once have I heard even a whisper of jealousy. We sensed that we were serving with a man immeasurably our superior.

As I see it, his outstanding characteristic was his clarity of vision and his power of shedding all unessentials from his thoughts, added to his uncanny knowledge of what the other man was thinking and doing.

Think of it! A young second lieutenant of the Egyptian Expeditionary Force goes down the Arabian coast to where a sporadic revolt of the Western Arabs had broken out against their Turkish masters. Then, with the help of a few British officers, all senior to himself, and professional soldiers, who willingly placed themselves under his general guidance, he galvanizes the Arab revolt into a coherent whole. By his daring courage, his strategy, his novel tactics, he welds the turbulent Arab tribes into a fighting machine of such value that he is able to immobilize two Turkish divisions and provide a flank force for Lord Allenby's final advance through Palestine and Syria, the value of which that great general acknowledged again and again...

What was it that enabled Lawrence to seize and hold the imagination of the Arabs? It is a difficult question to answer. The Arabs were noted individualists, intractable to a degree, and without any sense of discipline. Yet it was sufficient for almost any one of us to say that Lawrence wanted something done, and forthwith it was done.

How did he gain this power? The answer may partly be that he represented the heart of the Arab movement for freedom, and the Arabs realized that he had vitalized their cause; that he could do everything and endure everything just a little better than the Arabs themselves; that by his investment with the gold dagger of Mecca he ranked with the Ashraf or the descendants of the Prophet, and the Emir Feisal treated him as a brother and an equal.

But chiefly, I think, we must look for the answer in Lawrence's uncanny ability to sense the feelings of any group of men in whose company he found himself; his power to probe behind their minds and to uncover the well-springs of their actions.

Lawrence clearly had the necessary leadership qualities: the representative qualities admired by the Bedouin, such as courage, endurance and hardiness, and the generic qualities of enthusiasm, integrity and toughness or 'demandingness'. In terms of the Situational Approach, Lawrence had more knowledge of the Arabs – gathered from working in Iraq as an archaeologist – and he alone among the British officers with Feisal spoke Arabic. He also knew a lot more about the Turkish Army than they did. In the Group context, he had a clear vision of the *task*, together with an intuitive sense of the *group* and the *individual*, which enabled him to create a working *team* out of very disparate elements.

No one *elected* Lawrence as leader. His sole *appointment* was as Political Adviser to the Emir Feisal. But Lawrence had the necessary conditions for emerging as a strategic leader even in a field dominated by military hierarchy. And he had the sufficient condition – *phronesis*, practical wisdom, the mind of a strategic leader. Thus nine-tenths of Lawrence's success as a leader can be explained in terms of my general theory. But, last but not least, Lawrence also had an indefinable charisma, a tenth gene. He himself called it 'the irrational tenth, like the kingfisher flashing across the pool'.

The real innovation – symbolized by Athens in the 5th century BC – was the principle of free and equal citizens *electing* their leaders. It was a key ingredient in *democracy* – literally in Greek, rule by the people, especially a majority as opposed to *autocracy*, rule by one person with unlimited power, or *oligarchy* (a government in which a small group exercises control, especially for corrupt and selfish purposes). Democracy was in fact an urban form of the much older form of tribal life, where free and equal men had *leaders* – and families that produced leaders – but not *kings* who dominated them as masters. The Bedouin tribes of Lawrence's day and mine still reflected that culture.

Whether *democracy* in Greek cities was the least worst system or not was a matter of much debate – the demagogue made his first appearance in Athens. The word *demagogue* literally means 'people leading', and could range in meaning from a leader championing the cause of the common people (as Julius Caesar cleverly did in Rome) to one who makes use of popular prejudices and false claims and promises to gain power. Hitler was such a demagogue. In 1934 he was democrat-ically elected to power.

Hence the importance to Socrates and his companions of thinking through what makes a *good* leader, so that their intelligent fellow cit-izens might discern the difference between a persuasive demagogue and a true Pericles or Themistocles. *Elected* leaders tend to hold them-selves accountable to their electorate; *appointed* leaders are account-able primarily to those who appointed them to get the task done, and only secondarily, if at all, to their group. As both of these luminaries went off the boil as leaders – power tends to corrupt – democracy provides a system of getting rid of leaders without having to assassi-nate them. The principle of *election* implies that the best people to judge a person's leadership ability – their fitness for the role – are those that know him or her best, namely, in the context of Athens, the person's fellow citizens, or perhaps in our day those in the same work group. How do you do it?

THE PRINCIPLE OF ELECTION

A familiar form of election is to have a secret ballot or show of hands as a formal *vote*, as a trade union, political party, a club or society might do, the candidates having been either proposed and seconded or self-nominated. How good the resultant designated leader proves to be depends upon two factors: the leadership calibre of the candi-dates on offer and the judgement or wisdom of the electors. Ideally they need to know the persons concerned as individuals, and also have a clear idea of what they expect of a leader. They should not be like Shakespeare's 'distracted multitude':

> He's loved of the distracted multitude,
> Who like not in their judgement but in their eyes.

You see why at present leadership of political parties, like the Conservatives in the UK, is such a hit-or-miss affair. First, often *all* the candidates lack leadership (attribute). Each of them is, as Plutarch said of one Gaius Antonius, an elected Roman politician, 'a man with no aptitude for leadership in any direction, either good or bad'. Can political parties grow leaders?

The underlying model of a political party is that it is a collection or assembly of ambitious individuals all vying for cabinet-level jobs (*ambition* comes from a Latin verb for going around in order to canvass for votes). One's colleagues are seen either as competitors for office or – if you are party leader – actual or potential threats. Who would feed the sharks that one day will eat you?

A similar mindset is often present in organizations once one gets beyond a certain tree line in one's upward career. Then politics (with a small 'p') rears its ugly head. Political in-fighting is sometimes defended on Darwinian lines as promoting the survival of the fittest. As one manager who made it to the top wrote to me, not without a hint of self-satisfaction:

> The process of development that takes place in this company is rather like a steeplechase. As you jump over the various obstacles and challenges you build up your experience and stamina. Also the same race weeds out those who are unable to cope effectively.

Maybe. What your organization needs to check, however, is that those who reach the top are not merely the cunning, Machiavellian place-seekers who out-manoeuvre the remaining horses in the race, or apply their whips to a rival's face. Those who occupy roles of strategic leadership need to be the fittest for the role, not those best at head-office intrigue.

What the ideas in Part 1 should enable you to do is *to ask the right questions* in order to determine who deserves to be chosen for a leadership post on merit. Here are some suggestions – all three approaches that constitute the main body of knowledge about leadership:

■ Does he or she naturally contribute to enabling a group to achieve its task and to maintain it as a cohesive and harmonious working team? What is the evidence or data to support a positive answer? If task-focused, does he or she find time for teambuilding and for individuals?

■ Relative to the group or team he or she will be leading, does the person have the kind of professional knowledge/technical ability that will command respect? Does he or she have the relevant experience to qualify him or her to lead at this level?

■ Does the person exemplify the qualities required in and admired by those that he or she will be leading? Is there any issue about his or her enthusiasm or commitment, integrity or honesty, toughness or humanity, confidence or fairness? What additional qualities or characteristics have others noted in the person?

It is relatively easy to ask the right questions, much harder to get accurate answers. The clue is to look for *patterns of behaviour* – patterns that suggest present dispositions. If, for example, someone has shown themselves to have been calm, cool and collected in a series of stressful, dangerous or challenging situations *yesterday* or *today*, it is reasonable to deduce that they will probably act that way *tomorrow*. Not a mechanical certainty, true, but human nature doesn't allow for that kind of navigational exactitude. You are looking for probabilities, no more. 'Probabilities guide the decisions of wise men,' as Cicero once wisely said.

APPLYING THE GROUP OR FUNCTIONAL APPROACH TO FIRST-LINE LEADERSHIP SELECTION

The traditional method of selection where you do not know the person concerned is the *interview*. The natural or best way of selection, of course, is to know and observe the person over a period of time and in a variety of revealing if not testing situations. But when you are selecting someone for a team or operational leadership role from a shortlist of *outside* candidates you don't have that sort of knowledge.

You can see why wise organizations prefer to grow their own leaders. That is not an argument against outside appointments – all organizations benefit from fresh blood. Leadership potential is just not so hard to assess in those you have summered and wintered with.

There are no psychometric questionnaire-type tests that measure leadership. The real breakthrough in this area, as I have already mentioned once or twice, came during World War II in Britain.

At the outbreak of war in 1939 the British Army numbered about 900,000. Three years later that number had risen to some 3,000,000 men and women in khaki, with a further 2 million in the Royal Navy and Royal Air Force. The pre-war cadre of professional officers obviously provided the more senior levels of military leadership for these armed forces, but there was a massive demand – especially in the Army – for junior officers to command at platoon and company level.

Consequently, 13 Officer Training Units were established to produce the necessary officers, but there was a major problem: at times up to 50 per cent of soldiers sent there for training were being returned to their units as unfit to be officers. The selection system, based implicitly upon the assumption of the Qualities Approach and depending solely on the interview method to identify the elusive traits, was clearly inadequate. Something urgently needed to be done.

The solution to the problem was the introduction in 1941 of the War Officer Selection Board (WOSB). So successful was it as a method of identifying leadership potential that it has remained in use, subject to various changes and modifications, in all three British Armed Services to this day. Quite early in its history organizations as diverse as the Home Civil Service and the Church of England adopted and adapted the WOSB approach: it is the founder and grandparent of today's assessment centres.

Having considered and rejected the German Army's methods of officer selection, the War Office decided to innovate. The WOSB method was the brainchild of a creative group of senior British Army officers and some civilian psychologists enlisted to help. Apart from introducing various intelligence and aptitude tests the chief contribution of the latter was the Group Functional Approach.

In those days that theory was no more than a hypothesis: it lacked the Three Circles and it was not integrated with the other two approaches. Present in all working groups, it suggested, there are *two* areas of need: *task achievement* and *group cohesiveness*. Leaders meet these two areas of need. By putting candidates into 'leaderless groups' – small groups without an appointed leader – observers who knew what they were looking for should be able to spot those who were naturally inclined to work in those two areas.

The idea, incidentally, that one person could respond to both sets of need – *task* and *group* – was actually a step forward, a step taken as a direct outcome of war. Academic social psychologists and psychotherapists were still working on the hypothesis that groups needed *two* leaders, one for task and one for human relations, not unlike the differentiated roles of mother and father in a large family.

By a person's *group effectiveness* the psychologists meant:

1. The effective *level of his functioning*: of his ability to contribute towards the functional aspect of the common task by planning and organizing the available abilities, materials, time, etc.
2. His *group-cohesiveness* or ability to bind the group in the direction of the common task: to relate its members emotionally to each other and to the task.
3. His *stability* or ability to stand up to resistance and frustrations without serious impairment of 1) or 2) and the results of their interplay.

This specification was written by Dr Henry Harris in *The Group Approach to Leadership Testing* (Routledge & Kegan Paul, 1949). He started work with WOSB in 1943 and saw 6,000 candidates through the system before 1948 when he wrote his book. He added:

> 'Stability' is not a very dynamic term for what is essentially a dynamic concept, ie the active and continuous capacity not only to resist the deteriorating effects of stress, but also to return to normal when these have passed off... Mental stamina might do as a better word.

In short, Harris concluded, in the WOSB technique of officer selection, one observes a man faced with group-task in order to determine his group effectiveness (in a particular field): one selects and *tests* him *in* a group *for* a group.

When the British Army eventually stopped employing professional psychologists on the staffs of its WOSBs, the Group or Functional Approach as a conscious theory tended to sink into oblivion. 'Leaderless groups' were retained, as well as groups with appointed leaders, and military selectors continued to observe how individuals reacted in a group with a task to perform under time pressure. Indeed, so well designed was WOSB and its successors, that the absence of psychologists on site made little or no difference to its effectiveness as a selection tool.

On a personal note, as a candidate for a commission I attended a WOSB in 1953 and I remember being very impressed by it, not least its fairness. Titles, class, public school, family connections with a regiment, none of these counted – only merit. When in the 1960s I introduced the Group or Functional Approach into Sandhurst for *training* purposes, I was unaware that a prototype of the Three Circles – without the actual model – already lay behind this highly successful and well-established *selection* process. But this fact is clear in Harris's reflections on leadership:

> One may suggest provisionally that leadership is the measure and degree of an individual's ability to influence – and be influenced by – a group in the implementation of a common task. *This circumscribes three important aspects of leadership function: the individual, the group and the task; and indicates leadership as a functional relationship between these three basic variables.* [my italics]
>
> In respect of the first two, it can only be highly effective if based on a sensitive understanding of the group's needs and on the ability to be influenced by it. The leader who dominates and drives a group towards an end they do not seek is unlikely to retain his leadership: his domination is brittle and will stand little stress. In so far as he considers the needs and mobilises the initiative of every member in the group; in so far as he helps them towards the goal which will give the group its greatest satisfaction and provide every member of it with the profound gratification of effective participation on his own level, and at his optimum tempo... his leadership is more real, more flexible, more resistant to stress, and incidentally more democratic – in the best sense of the word – than any leadership which is insensitive to the group in which it is exercised.

As I mentioned, the WOSB approach proved to be the inspiration of all latter-day assessment centres; not, of course, that they retained the original Group or Functional leadership theory behind WOSB.

Setting up and running a WOSB-type selection system is a very expensive business, justified in wartime or if you have very large numbers of candidates to deal with (WOSB assessed more than 1,000 a year), especially where the public interest called for a system that was both fair and seen to be fair. Still, large organizations that recruit graduates or equivalents as potential leaders would be wise to include some *group effectiveness* exercises – many do.

In retrospect, the WOSB was a beautiful design, and it reflects credit on the team who created it under the overall direction of the exceptional Adjutant General of the day, Sir Ronald Adam. It was *high volume, high quality* and *low cost*.

SELECTION – THE WIDER FRAMEWORK

You may have noticed that as leaders move up the natural team-operational-strategic hierarchy the quality of the *minds* – what T E Lawrence called *brainy leadership* – becomes ever more important. So, too, do their abilities as a *communicator* and their capacity to manage their time effectively.

Some people try to lump all these aspects into the concept of *leadership*, but I believe that it is clearer to regard them as separate concepts or concept-clusters. Using Douglas McGregor's phrase, 'the human side of enterprise' as the name for the particular part of the universe I wanted to chart, my first three books – *Training for Leadership* (Macdonald & Jane, 1968), *Training for Decisions* (Macdonald & Jane, 1969) and *Training for Communication* (Macdonald & Jane, 1973) – mapped out what was then known about these subjects and how – if at all – they could be best taught to learning leaders. Later I covered the fourth subject with *How to Manage Your Time* (Talbot Adair, 1987).

Thus, when asserting someone's potential as a leader you should be considering him or her against a set of neighbour-concepts:

- Leadership and teamwork, including qualities of personality and character, such as energy, enthusiasm and initiative.
- Decision-making; thinking skills in the applied forms of problem-solving, decision-making, and creative or innovative thinking.
- Communication skills (speaking, listening, writing, and reading; meetings); communicating in organizations.
- Self-management; the ability to organize oneself; time-management skills; learning skills.

This simple framework became the germ for others to develop lists of *leadership competencies*. It became a cottage industry for management consultants. I led the way in 1988 by publishing the results of my research into the lists of qualities/abilities identified by BOC, STC, British Rail, an IBM colloquium of industrialists on 'Preparing Tomorrow's Leaders', a London Borough, the Civil Service Selection Board, May & Baker, Shell, and some assessment centres. Bearing in mind my own chart of the celestial heavens, I grouped them under five headings.

1. Leadership and teamwork abilities

The ability to get things going – especially the ability to get people working well as a team towards a common goal. Typical behaviours:

- Sets direction and initiates action.
- Plans and organizes.
- Delegates responsibility.
- Coordinates and controls.
- Shows sensitivity to needs and feelings of individuals.
- Motivates and encourages others.
- Sets group standards.
- Disciplines where necessary.
- Seeks help and advice.
- Plays positive role as team member.

2. Decision-making abilities

The ability to think clearly in order to be able to solve problems and make decisions. Typical behaviours:

- Analyses problems.
- Shows reasoning and logical thinking.
- Is 'swift on the uptake'.
- Thinks imaginatively and creatively.
- Has a sense of reality.
- Has 'helicopter' ability to stand back.
- Demonstrates good judgement.
- Has an inquiring mind.
- Generates solutions.
- Is decisive when required.

3. Communication abilities

The ability to make points so that others understand them, and to comprehend the points that others make. Typical behaviours:

- Speaks audibly and clearly.
- Uses simple and concise language.
- Communicates on paper easily and well.
- Listens to others with perception.
- Reads with speed and comprehension.
- Argues assertively but not aggressively.
- Chairs a meeting well.
- Ensures good group communications, upwards, downwards and sideways.
- Shows awareness of non-verbal communication.
- Gets others enthusiastic about his ideas.

4. Self-management abilities

The ability to manage your time effectively and to organize yourself well. Typical behaviours:

- A self-motivator – 'lights his or her own fire'.
- Able to work on own initiative with little supervision.
- Sets and achieves challenging goals.
- Works to deadlines.
- Makes good use of his or her own time.

5. Personal qualities

The following qualities (in no order of merit) are mentioned as being of value by employers of graduates:

- Enthusiasm.
- Integrity.
- Strong but not dominating personality.
- Personal impact, good appearance, poise.
- Resilience, ability to work under pressure.
- Flexibility and adaptability.

■   Energy and vigour.
■   Self-confidence or self-assurance.
■   Reliability, stability, calmness.
■   Breadth of interest.

Some useful support for this wider framework came from the Institute of Manpower Studies in that same year.

Wendy Hirsh and Stephen Bevan, in *What Makes a Manager?* (Institute of Manpower Studies, 1991), surveyed over 40 organizations in all sectors: *leadership, intellectual attributes and conceptual skills,* and *communication* (oral and general) came top of the list. They commented, however:

> Although a 'national skill language' appears to exist in terms of some very common expressions in use, we cannot infer that these terms have a common meaning in different organizations. In fact, some of the commonest skill items, such as *leadership*, are used with the most diverse meanings.

The corporate practice of listing 'skills' (later 'competencies' took over as the preferred term) was a definite step forwards in the right direction. In 1988 Hirsh and Bevan already identified as *good practice* those organizational lists with the following characteristics:

■   relatively short and simple lists of skills are used;
■   skill descriptions are couched, wherever possible, in terms of specific behaviour which can be observed, rather than in more abstract terms;
■   skill languages are made as similar in style and format as possible ('harmonized') across groups of managers (functions, levels, etc) and across human resources processes (recruitment, assessment, management training programmes, etc);
■   consistent understanding of skill terminology is further assisted by appraisal and selection training, and experience of group assessment or group discussion (in assessment centres, succession planning committees, etc).

If your organization has produced a set of *leadership competencies* in living memory, you may like to compare it against that sketch of *good practice.* How would you rate the current NHS list, shown below?

A Successful Leader...

■ Communicates clear vision, direction, and roles.
■ Strategically influences and engages others.
■ Builds relationships.
■ Challenges thinking and encourages flexibility and innovation.
■ Develops, enables, and encourages others.
■ Drives for results and improvement.
■ Practices political astuteness.
■ Displays self-awareness.
■ Commits with passion to values and mission.
■ Demonstrates mastery of management skills.

Lists such as these are intended to be used for *selection* purposes, both at recruitment and at promotion levels, as well as *training* and *appraising*. Don't, however, take them too seriously. Although they often cost the human resources department a large sum to produce them, their fate is to be put away in the bottom drawer of the manager's filing cabinet – just as back in 1953 I filed away the British Army's list of 17 leadership qualities/competencies.

Compilers of leadership competencies, of course, have not been working from first principles as I have, nor have they shown any knowledge of the progress in our understanding of leadership which I have outlined above. The notion of management (and leadership) competence seems to have originated with the work of the McBer management consultancy firm for the American Management Association in the late 1970s. A competency was defined as an underlying characteristic of a person that results in effective or superior performance in a job.

The method used was to generate a list of competencies from analysis of numerous managers' jobs in a particular organization or field – an averaging out of multiple individuals. The result is an overpowering list of qualities. The ill-starred Council for Excellence in Management Leadership in 2001 identified 83 management and leadership attributes, condensed from a list of over 2,000! By contrast, my approach is to work from the simple to the complex.

All that you do need to know – it is easy to remember – is the generic role of *leadership*, together with the essentials of the *intellec-*

tual, communication and *time-management* clusters. Everything else, when judging leaders or would-be leaders, falls under the heading of the fitness of their *professional or technical knowledge*. At present I cannot make it simpler than that. What have I left out?

Key points

- Growing leaders is not easy. Why not select people for leadership roles who already have a rich potential for leadership within them?

- Natural selection of leaders needs to be understood. Leaders are *emergent, elected* or *appointed*, or some combination of the three. A British prime minister emerges in his or her party, is elected by colleagues or party, and appointed by the Queen.

- Difficulty arises when electors or selectors lack first-hand knowledge of a candidate for a leadership role. The Qualities, Situational and Group or Functional Approaches taken together provide the necessary criteria.

- The Group or Functional Approach worked well in leadership *selection*. The WOSB method solved problems distinctive to the military field, but the underlying principle remains relevant today for assessing leadership potential.

- *Leadership* has neighbouring concepts living in the same street: the *intellectual, communication* and *self-management* galaxies of skills, qualities and abilities.

- Eclectic lists of 'competencies' drawn from these four constellations have value. But they need to be kept *short* and *simple*, which inevitably makes them more generic in nature.

- If an organization doesn't understand the key concept of leadership and its associated terms, it should not expect to be wise in its choice of leaders.

Nobody doubted his capacity to rule until he became Emperor.
Tacitus, writing about Galba

PRINCIPLE THREE

Line Managers as Leadership Mentors

One other thing stirs me when I look back at my youthful days, the fact that so many people gave me something or were something to me without knowing it.

Albert Schweitzer

Before we begin I should unpack some of the words above. The military distinction between *line* and *staff* is, I believe, both transferable and useful. Over-simplifying it, the *line* does the work, while the *staff* performs a supporting function – administration, supplies, logistics, human resources and maybe specialist or technical advice. The line of command – or as we would say, the principal line of communication – runs as a two-way dialogue between strategic, operational and team leaders.

Incidentally, that dialogue up and down the line doesn't always run through the operational leadership level as the channel of communication. A general can talk directly to the soldiers, and vice-versa. What is important, however, is that when it comes to the giving of instructions the commander-in-chief obeys the established principle of *respecting the line*, that is, asking the operational leader to act. Thereby the trust of the operational leaders is not forfeited.

WHAT IS A MENTOR?

A mentor is a guide, a wise and trusted counsellor. The word comes from Mentor, a friend of Ulysses entrusted with the education of his son Telemachus. It was his bodily form the goddess Athene, according to the story, assumed when she accompanied Telemachus in his search for his father. Homer probably chose the name because it echoes a Greek root meaning 'remember, think, counsel'.

The principle above, then, suggests that in part – fulfilment of the *individual* circle needs – line leaders should act as teachers of the apprentice – line leaders who happen to be in their team. And this learning process – the apprentice-method – should happen at all levels. Let me show you the principle at work.

ON-THE-JOB TRAINING

General Horrocks recalled one incident that revealed Montgomery's ability to develop the individual, even at the higher levels of leadership.

'On the day after the battle [Alam Halfa] I was sitting in my headquarters purring with satisfaction. The battle had been won and I had not been mauled in the process. What could be better? Then in came a liaison officer from 8th Army headquarters bringing me a letter in Monty's even hand. This is what he said:

'"Dear Horrocks,

'"Well done – but you must remember that you are now a corps commander and not a divisional commander..."

'He went on to list four or five things that I had done wrong, mainly because I had interfered too much with the tasks of my subordinate commanders. The purring stopped abruptly.

'Perhaps I wasn't such a heaven-sent general after all. But the more I thought over the battle, the more I realised that Monty was right. So I rang him up and said, "Thank you very much."

'I mention this because Montgomery was one of the few commanders who tried to train the people who worked under him. Who else, on the day after his first major victory, which had altered the whole complexion of the war in the Middle East, would have taken the trouble to write a letter like this in his own hand to one of his subordinate commanders?'

Lieutenant General Sir Brian Horrocks, *A Full Life* (Collins, 1956)

Look back on your own career as a leader. Can you identify anyone that you worked for who found time for you as an *individual*? Who showed interest in helping you to grow as a leader, and shared their experience with you to that end?

THE APPRENTICESHIP METHOD

Apprenticeship is the traditional method of learning an art, craft or trade. A would-be practitioner articles himself – formally or informally – to a master-craftsman, and in return for a very modest wage (and in the Middle Ages bed-and-board) he worked alongside the master. The master's role was to show by example, but also to instruct, explain or teach as well. A good master, especially if he spied real aptitude in the apprentice, would encourage as well, like any good teacher. Apprentice comes from the Latin *apprendere*, to learn.

If apprenticeship is the natural way of growing leaders, then organizations that want to grow leaders should work with it. Now there is a better vocabulary for conversation between line leaders and their apprentices. Not that intellectual discussions about leadership matters a fig. What matters is seeing it done and having the opportunity to ask questions.

CASE STUDY: THE COMMANDO LEADER

The Army was not my career choice – I was conscripted – but I aspired to be a military leader. Joining the Arab Legion in Jerusalem in 1954 opened up a new world to me, for I found myself an apprentice to a master-commander, one who was willing to teach me the trade. Peter Young, colonel of the Ninth Bedouin Regiment, had won a DSO and three Military Crosses as a Commando leader in World War II, becoming a brigadier-general at the age of 26. Peter made me his Adjutant (a captain's appointment), despite protests from his brigade superior that I was too young (20) for the job. He exemplified excellence as a regimental leader. *Leadership is done from in front* summed up Peter's philosophy. A natural teacher, he treated me as an equal, a partner in the common enterprise.

An apprentice, then, is a learner of a craft, bound to serve, and *entitled to instruction* from his or her employer for a specified time. I have sketched above my own apprentice-hood. If you look carefully at the careers of outstanding leaders in any field, you usually find that they learnt most about leadership not from courses or books but by serving their apprenticeship with a master-leader. You should not assume that leadership mentors are always senior to you in the hierarchy: it is as if Athene sometimes speaks to you through those who are inferior in rank.

CASE STUDY: LYNDAL URWICK

Urwick was a leading British thinker on the theory of management practice, one of the few to be recognized as a prophet of modern management techniques in the USA. He established one of the earliest firms of management education and training in this country. He virtually founded the Administrative Staff College at Henley (now Henley Management College), and he played a major role in the foundation of the British Institute of Management (now Chartered Management Institute).

Urwick served in World War I, gaining a Military Cross. In a letter to me about *Training for Leadership* in 1969 he described how just after leaving Oxford he had found himself in August 1914 as a junior subaltern in a line battalion.

'A year later, owing to casualties, I was its senior Captain commanding a Company at the tip of the Ypres Salient. I blush with shame to look back on what an arbitrary young fool I often was. But I was saved, sustained and – I hope – educated by my Company Sergeant Major. He was a regular of about 12 to 15 years service. He had been a Band Sergeant, so he understood boys. He had also been Orderly Room Sergeant, so he understood about the paper work. I have always counted him one of the best men I ever knew. Alas, he was killed at Thiepval the following summer commanding the selfsame Company as Acting Captain.'

Urwick was never to forget the teaching on how to be a leader that he received from that unnamed CSM. He was one of the first to lecture and write on leadership. The British Institute of Management, formed in 1948, took as its motto *Ducere est Servire*, To Lead is to Serve. The strap-line of its successor today is 'Inspiring Leaders'.

Being realistic, most line managers do not give any one-to-one mentoring to individual members of their team, including their apprentice-leaders. But growing leaders need that one-to-one attention. Therefore a growing number of organizations are paying professional mentors to fill the leadership vacuum.

Such professional mentors – I act as one to a chief executive myself – often provide a valuable function as a sounding board. A sounding board is a structure above a pulpit, rostrum or platform to give distinctiveness and sonority to the sound uttered from it. Following the metaphor, a modern mentor helps the client by listening to them think something through – to hear their own voice.

Leadership as such – conversations with leadership implicitly or explicitly as the subject – is not on the agenda. David Clutterbuck's *Everyone Needs a Mentor: Fostering Talent in Your Organization* (CIPD, 4th edn, 2004) has only one brief and passing reference to leadership.

The reason is not surprising. The outside professional mentor is unable to observe the client at work as a leader; the mentor, not usually having experience as a leader, is not the sort of person the client could learn leadership from. In other words, the relationship lacks the necessary conditions for it to provide *leadership* mentoring. If you want that, look inside your organization and persuade team, operational and strategic leaders to start doing the job for which they are being paid. How do you do that? Here are some suggestions:

- Do some detective work and discover one or two operational leaders among those in your team who are, a) as busy as any, and b) yet find time to bring on their apprentice leaders.
- Organize a two-hour meeting before a buffet supper for operational and team leaders, where those chosen can talk for 20 minutes or so about how they go about it. Then open it to general discussion.
- If you can add a perspective from another organization – one recognized for best practice – so much the better.
- Always speak briefly yourself, explaining that it is part of *your* role to ensure that this organization maximizes every bit of leadership potential in it and at every level. Point out the obvious, namely that you cannot do it by yourself, but you are counting on every operational and team leader in the room to play their part.

AT LEAST YOU CAN SAY 'GOODBYE'

In all relations there is a bare minimum. In a leadership role if you drop below the bare minimum, then you are… well, just a liability. Setting the *task* and *team* circles on one side, in the *individual* circle – the *developing* dimension of it – the bare minimum is to see the team member before they go on a leadership course or programme and to see them again after their return.

You can do that by going through the motions as a drill, just to keep the system happy, but I don't advocate that. If you approach it as a leader the picture soon begins to change and to come alive. The apprenticeship model I have been advocating may start out as a teacher-learner one, but as it progresses it becomes more a learner-learner one. The master-craftsman is always open to learning, for as

G K Chesterton said, 'only the secure are humble'. The master-leader teaches by learning.

CASE STUDY: THE LEARNING COMPANY

Bill Henderson, a departmental head in a large pharmaceutical company, told me that two of his eight team leaders have just been on one of my ACL courses.

'Have the two others who have gone on it benefited?' I inquired. 'If so, how?'

'I think so,' he said, 'I had enthusiastic e-mails from three of them, thanking the human resources department for nominating them.'

'So you did not suggest the course to them in person, as part of their leadership development?' I asked.

'No,' he replied. 'In this company training comes under the director of human resources.'

'Didn't you see each of them before they went on the courses, stressing the importance of good leadership, relating the course objectives to their needs and fixing a date for a debrief afterwards?'

Bill laughed. 'Come off it, John. Now we are launching GXR3 we are so busy that I don't have the time for that sort of thing. I did meet them in the corridor about a week ago and told them to enjoy their holiday, as we were going to be flat out for the next three months.'

Bill is a highly knowledgeable biochemist, but he is missing out on a whole circle in the Three Circles model. The lessons are as follows:

■ Bill, as an operational lower-level leader, owns the problem of developing his eight team leaders; it is not the problem of the human resources training department. They are in a *staff* relation to him; there to give specialist advice on, for example, what training courses to send them on.

▪ He should brief the team leaders individually (remember that *briefing* is a key leadership function, and it applies to individuals as well as to the team). There the *intentions* and *expected benefits* should be covered. Above all, he should convey the importance or worthwhileness of becoming a better leader – it is a real opportunity to enthuse if not inspire.

▪ After the course there should be a debrief on a one-to-one basis, covering:
  - What have you learnt?
  - How do you intend you apply it in your team context?
  - How can I help you?
  - What wider lessons did you learn which might benefit the department or the company?
  - What more training do you need?

▪ Three months later, Bill should check progress and give some further encouragement, for initial enthusiasm after a course can soon fade if no more fuel is put on the fire.

▪ Lastly, Bill needs to give the human resources/training specialist some feedback on the value of the team leadership course they recommended.

In fact I knew Bill Henderson quite well, and saw real potential in him as a leader. He telephoned me the day after our conversation, just to say that my comments had made him think hard. We then talked through the points I have listed above.

About three months later I met him again by chance while awaiting a flight at Gatwick. He assured me that he had followed my advice with the remaining four team leaders. The difference in their initial motivation and in the post-course results had been spectacular. 'I can see now that you are really interested in my leadership,' the youngest and last appointed team leader had told him, 'and that makes me care about it too.'

After a cup of coffee, Bill added: 'One other thing, John. I went to one of the chief executive's "Master-classes in Leadership" as he called them, which he said was based on one of your books. It was about line managers as leadership mentors. Four or five days later the eight team leaders went off to a local hotel for a planning session. We rounded it off with a working supper, and I shared with them what I had learnt at the master-class. We have agreed to meet again just before Christmas to share things that we are learning about leadership, from our own experience or what we see going on. We are also going to e-mail any key points about leading or managing we pick up from books – a kind of poor man's master-class if you like.'

'To Lead is to Serve.' If you take nothing else away from this book take away that motto, which today I rescued from the dustbin of history for *you*.

Part of your service is to help your team grow, both as a group and as individuals; this will not happen if you don't find time to spend with them individually. As the Japanese proverb has it, 'If he works for you, you work for him.'

Often you will be ploughing and sowing seeds, but others will reap the harvest. Occasionally, you will have the joy of knowing that something you said or wrote, a half-forgotten meeting years ago, has proved to be decisive in someone else's inner journey. Athene paid Mentor in the coinage of joy.

At a crisis in my youth, he taught me the wisdom of choice, to try and fail is at least to learn; to fail to try is to suffer the inestimable loss of what might have been.

Chester Barnard

Key points

■ A mentor is a wise and trusted guide or counsellor, one who helps a person to grow in his or her role and responsibilities. A good leader begets leaders: they are natural leadership mentors.

■ The natural way of learning leadership is 'on the job' – by practice – like an apprenticeship indentured to a master-artist, craftsman or practitioner. In this relationship the master is expected – it is part of the role – to give instruction. Why don't you teach the 'leaders for tomorrow' who work with you?

■ 'Under the banyan tree nothing grows.' As this Indian proverb suggests, some so-called 'great leaders' stunt the growth of those around them. It is only by making others great that a leader becomes great.

■ Line leaders as leadership mentors is a principle, not a system. It is a natural process, as old as mankind, so it doesn't need to be organized – merely encouraged. If you set an example as chief executive, it will happen as day follows night.

■ Occasionally, your positive influence will have come at a decisive time, and a person anxious about leading will suddenly find a new confidence in themselves and an eagerness to accept the leadership challenge.

■ The best teachers are also learners. As Chaucer wrote of one of his pilgrims: 'Gladly would he teach and gladly learn.' There is no point in talking if you don't listen.

It is the province of knowledge to speak, and it is the privilege of wisdom to listen.

Oliver Wendell Holmes

PRINCIPLE FOUR

The Chance to Lead

The only way in which the growing need for leadership in management can be met is to find the potential leader and then start his training and give him the chance to lead.

Lord Slim

As you will by now doubtless have guessed, the title of this book, *How to Grow Leaders,* is something of a misnomer. Organizations cannot grow leaders. It is nature or God that grows leaders. All that organizations do is to provide some of the necessary conditions for growth, and chief among them is *the opportunity to lead*.

Under that principle is gathered not just the initial (team leader) opportunity to lead, but a set of progressive steps or challenges throughout your career that educate – literally in Latin 'to lead out from you' – all the leadership that is within you. It is giving people who merit it the chance to lead.

THE MILITARY ANALOGY

You can see the principle clearly at work when nations go to war for protracted periods of time, as in World War I and II. Their armies expand – you recollect that the British Army grew from about 300,000 in 1936 to over 3 million in 1944. A set of progressive steps or challenges – opportunities to lead ever larger bodies of men in challenging circumstances – suddenly is there for young military leaders who are ready, willing and able to take these unexpected opportunities. In the last chapter, for example, I mentioned Peter Young, a Commando brigadier (4,000 men) at the age of 26 years. If a war lasts for years, then casualties, accidents and retirements increase the opportunity level.

This proliferation of strategic leadership opportunities looks for leaders, but it is also true that they grow the strategic leader. Remove World War I and there would have been no Lawrence of Arabia. Remove World War II and Winston Churchill, Montgomery, Slim, Eisenhower and Rommel would be names unknown to us.

It is worth pausing to reflect for a moment on just how dependent leaders are upon the chance to lead. My *John Hampden: The Patriot* (Thorogood, 2003) is the biography of a country gentleman who was the first commoner to emerge as the national leader of England, but it took the upheaval of the English Civil War to make that possible. Without it his great powers of leadership would have remained latent. I was married in Stoke Poges Church, in whose famous churchyard the poet Thomas Gray wrote his elegy on those unknown 'forefathers' who lacked the chance to lead:

Full many a flower is born to blush unseen,
And waste its sweetness on the desert air.
Some village – Hampden, that with dauntless breast
The little tyrant of his fields withstood;
Some mute inglorious Milton here may rest,
Some Cromwell guiltless of his country's blood.

You can see why it is difficult for peacetime armies with limited experience of active service to grow military leaders. The opportunities just aren't there. The danger was that when war came, the process of trial-and-error in finding military leaders who can lead at strategic level could be so protracted that victory could be won by an enemy with fewer resources but better leaders. The North almost lost the American Civil War while Lincoln struggled to find generals who could match the leadership of Robert E Lee and 'Stonewall' Jackson.

WHAT CAN ORGANIZATIONS DO?

Organizations, it follows, that are growing in size and expanding globally have a further competitive advantage in having more leadership opportunities to offer their managers – real challenges for business strategic leaders.

Conversely, organizations that are contracting in size and scope, pulling in their horns and retreating into their shells, have far fewer opportunities in their gift, so they will find it correspondingly much more difficult to grow leaders.

You notice here the elements of a chicken-and-egg problem. It is business leaders who grow businesses; growing businesses grow leaders. Leaders may downsize or de-layer organizations, or rationalize their products and services, but it is still 'growth' if they are *pruning or cutting back with growth in mind*. They have a vision of what this organization is going to be in five years time, and it is that vision which recruits others leaders – younger ones eager to grow or progress with the organization. As you know, leadership is a journey word – no journey, no leader.

WHAT CONSTITUTES A CHALLENGE?

'Challenge' is a somewhat overused word these days, but there is no doubt that true leaders love a challenge. From the organization's viewpoint, if you can provide a young leader with a challenge and help him or her to meet it, then you have in effect grown a leader. But the challenge level has to be at the optimum level: not *too* difficult and not *too* easy. In other words, it has to be *stretching*.

> High sentiments always win in the end. The leaders who offer blood, toil, tears and sweat always get more out of their followers than those who offer safety and a good time. When it comes to the pinch, human beings are heroic.
>
> (George Orwell, *Collected Essays,* Secker & Warburg, 1970)

Optimum response will only be produced by a challenge of optimum severity. Frederick Hooper, an experienced business leader had these wise words to say on the subject in *Management Survey* (Penguin, 1959):

> Too severe a challenge will overwhelm; one insufficiently severe will evoke an insufficient response with too little impetus behind it. There is not, and cannot be, any easy interpretation of a golden rule.
>
> Moreover we have to recognize that a challenge which may have proved too severe at one point of a man's development might prove to be the optimum at another and later stage in his career when the man himself may, by attaining to a new internal balance in his qualities, have become to all practical purposes a new man. The continuing development of a career not infrequently follows a series of steps describing what is virtually a half-circle, each step a tangent, setting off at a slight angle form the one that preceded it, and yet dependent upon the latter for its due starting point. Steps are seldom retraced; thus past and present experience offers in such a case little obvious indication of what may prove to be the right step for the future, and any attempt to base prediction upon the evidence of the past may well be actively misleading. Nor can one safely make the assumption, however much assisted by the best of selection systems, that a man can save himself the journey of the circle and somehow cut straight across from A to Z. The weight of evidence is too heavily to the contrary.

Leaders often comment on the thrill of challenge, of accepting a task that may seem a *mission impossible*. 'There is no greater joy in life,' the inventor Barnes Wallis said, 'than first proving a thing is impossible and then showing how it can be done.' The leader of the first expedition to conquer Everest, John Hunt, also spoke of that first taste of a challenge: 'Some of the best moments in life are not when you have achieved something but when the thought first comes to you to have a go.'

A challenge is literally a summons, often threatening, provocative, stimulating or exciting. The old biblical word for a summons was *call*, hence our words *calling* and (in its Latin form) *vocation*. God called you to a piece of work. But, as Genesis has it, the 'word' of God is His creative instrument. So, putting it in our language, a true challenge is also a creative one. Moses was presented with a seemingly impossible task. He felt himself not to be up to it. But he said yes and he grew as a leader – it was a creative experience. He did have one asset – humility – which meant that he was willing to listen to good advice.

CASE STUDY: CREATING A SIMPLE STRUCTURE

Structure, organization, hierarchy and communication are four different ways of saying the same thing. When a group grows too large it has to sub-divide, and that creates a hierarchy.

Moses in the wilderness at first attempted to lead the 12 tribes of Israel as if he were a team leader. One day his father-in-law Jethro watched him as he sat alone all day from dawn to dusk listening to complaints, resolving disputes and giving counsel. 'This is not the best way to do it,' said Jethro. 'You will only wear yourself out and wear out all the people who are here. The task is too heavy for you; you cannot do it by yourself. Now listen to me...'

Jethro told him that he must remain the people's representative before God and to instruct them in the principles of how to behave and what to do. 'But you must yourself search for capable, God-fearing men among all the people, honest and incorruptible men, and appoint them over the people as officers over units of a thousand, of a hundred, of 50 or 10. They shall sit as a permanent court for the people; they must refer difficult cases to you but decide simple cases themselves. In this way your burden will be lightened, and they will share it with you. If you do this, moreover, this whole people will here and now regain peace and harmony.'

Moses, who is described elsewhere as a 'very meek man', listened to his father-in-law and did all that he suggested.

FORTUNE FAVOURS THE PREPARED MIND

As a general principle, the longer that you have to prepare for a challenge the more likely you are to rise to it. If you or I had to run the New York marathon next week we might struggle – me more than you. But give yourself six months and you would do fine. As for me, well, even the snail finally made it to the Ark.

We cannot foresee in our careers the specific challenges that (we hope) await us, but it makes sense to look ahead to the *type* of challenges that will appeal, and for which – in a general way – we can obey the Scout motto and Be Prepared.

That means, of course, that you must 'think and think until it really hurts' about your vocation. What is your talent? Which direction do you want to take? The basic question to ask yourself is: 'Am I in the right field?'

This is territory I explore in *How to Find Your Vocation* (Canterbury Press, 2003). If you have found your vocation – the work you love to do – I would say that you are already quite far down the track of becoming a leader. You will already be developing the qualities or attributes required and admired in your field. That morning star of a generic leadership quality – *enthusiasm* – is already in the bag. Becoming a leader in your field is a second vocation.

The second question, then, is: 'Do I want that "second calling" to leadership?' Maybe you are content to remain an individual contributor in your chosen field. Here it is helpful to bear in mind my model of a leader's typical course. It looks like an hourglass or egg-timer, as shown in the following diagram.

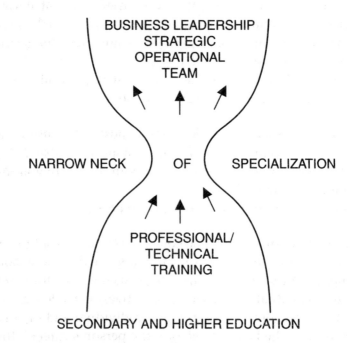

The hourglass model of career change

As you can see, you move from the general to the particular, and you usually 'make your name' as a specialist. You can either stay in the narrow neck of specialization with a career like an inverted funnel, or you can broaden out and become a generalist again. One eye surgeon may want to 'stick to the last' and perfect her skill by focusing on practice; another eye surgeon may sense that becoming the chief executive of a NHS Hospital Trust is the path of his vocation. No moral value separates the two paths: both are forms of service. It is principally a matter of interest, aptitude and temperament.

Institute an annual career review

Perceptions about careers change. An individual who has been content to be a specialist may discover that he or she is looking for a fresh challenge. Organizations, for their part, need to think about the careers of their employees for a different reason: they have slots to fill in the existing hierarchy and – if the organization is growing and spreading its wings – they are looking for new leaders.

If you haven't done so already, set up a system so that at least once a year there is a summit meeting between the individual – specialist, line manager, staff manager, employee – and the organization, or rather its mandated representative.

The organization needs to *listen* to what individuals are saying about what they aspire to do in their careers:

■ Do you want to be, in the widest sense of business, a business leader?
■ If you wish to remain a specialist, what are your goals?
■ Are you looking forward to staying with us, or are you thinking of moving elsewhere?
■ Would you be interested in working overseas?

Equally, the individuals have the chance to *listen* to what the organization has in store for them – if anything. In the succession plan (assuming, of course, there is one – see Principle Six), for what positions is the individual concerned being actively considered?

The perfect outcome, of course, is if individual and organization agree on what is the best next step in the person's career – the win-win situation being best for both parties. Then some agreed steps can be taken to prepare a person for the change ahead. What are the gaps in their professional or technical knowledge? Are there any general leadership programmes that will help to make them promotable?

What the organization cannot do, however, is to infringe Principle Two. In other words, the organization, say a large civil engineering company, should not tell you in advance that you will be the next operational leader in charge of building Terminal Five at London Heathrow Airport. The person chosen from the shortlist for that post will be the best construction leader for the job, and may be an outside candidate. What it can and should do is to work with the individual concerned to enable them to get on that particular shortlist – or its successors – by merit alone.

If we go back to the Three Circles model, the circles overlap but there is a tension between them. Not a conflict – for then there would be no overlap – but a tension. There is, for example, a tension between the needs of the *individual* and the needs of the *group* (or, group writ large, the *organization*). That tension may become a conflict, in which case the individual is free to withdraw and go elsewhere, just as the organization is free to dispense with the services of any individual, even the chief executive. As the Scottish proverb says, 'The clan is greater than the chief.'

But it can be a creative tension. If communication between the *individual* and the organization is good, and there is a high level of mutual respect and trust (see Principle Six), then sometimes a risk can be taken in making a promotion. If it doesn't work out, both parties are flexible enough to think again.

With the best will in the world, organizations cannot always provide the perfect opportunity that a particular person might need to grow as a leader. The daily business has to be done – the *task* always has priority. But it remains an ideal to strive for: opportunity and practice are the natural parents of leadership. All that training (or education) does is to prepare us to act.

Key points

■ Leaders grow by facing and surmounting even more difficult leadership challenges. If organizations want to grow leaders – or at least create the conditions necessary for growth – they can do no better than to give potential leaders *the chance to lead*.

■ That opportunity should be accomplished by practical help in the form of training and support. Training for leadership dramatically increases the likelihood of success. Learner-leaders at any level benefit from having a leader above them who can encourage and support.

■ Individual and organization should put their heads together at least once a year to compare notes on 'career development' or promotion. If expectations can be matched and married, then there is harmony between the two sets of needs.

■ We all need challenges in order to grow, not least leaders. 'By asking the impossible we obtain the best possible', says the Italian proverb. Stretching is painful, but it is the only way to gain stature.

■ Not all specialists want to become generalists – leaders in their field. Those who do, however, need to think ahead and to prepare for tomorrow's opportunities.

■ It is an error to think that promotion is the only way to grow as a leader. It is better to achieve excellence as a team leader than to sink to mediocrity at operational level.

Responsibility is the great developer of men.

Mary Parker Follett

PRINCIPLE FIVE

Education for Leadership

It takes a whole society to raise a leader.

African proverb

The theme of this book is *how to grow leaders*. But, as I have said, leaders are not colleagues or cattle, and organizations are not leader-farms. Somehow or other individuals acquire the ability and confidence to lead. Organizations can create some necessary or at least useful conditions for that growth, such as careful selection, training and, above all, providing chances to lead. But organizations cannot grow leaders.

What my work at Sandhurst in the 1960s established beyond doubt is that the intervention of *training* – a carefully-balanced practical two-day course focusing on the generic role of leader and the need to develop skill in its component functions – had a decisive effect on this natural process of growth, provided that the course was properly conducted. If you like, it added an intellectual gene to the young natural leader's gene-bank, a compass that would guide all subsequent self-learning or self-development. Much of my career has been spent trying to persuade non-military organizations to provide similar courses at team leadership level.

But at Sandhurst I was aware, as I have already written, that *education* for military leadership was a much wider process than *training* for leadership. Indeed, the whole ethos of Sandhurst, in addition to its military and academic curriculum, was about becoming a military leader. If you doubt me, look back at the Queen's speech at Sandhurst in 1966 (see page 22).

You will notice, however, that in *Training for Leadership* (Macdonald & Jane, 1968) I still restricted this wider education for leadership to Sandhurst. Later, I also tried to persuade other organizations or professions that they, too, should have cultures and a strategic focus on the aim of developing leadership that Sandhurst exemplified. Now that it is much clearer that we are talking about the same generic role of leader, it is no longer necessary for me to persuade. The door is no longer locked. As Sophocles said, 'The truth is always the strongest argument.'

Yet my mind was imprisoned in a mental box called 'organization' and I needed to break out of it. Let me explain what I mean.

THINKING OUTSIDE THE BOX

Sandhurst itself was a mental box in the 1960s, a world on its own. The 'box' was an exceptionally pleasant one, for the pink-white building of Old College and its neighbours stood in their own extensive grounds, training areas and firing ranges. There was no contact with the civilian world of organizations and management development. Outside, the movement to transform British management education by establishing at great cost business schools on the Harvard model – notably the London Business School and the Manchester Business School – might have been happening on Mars: the British Army was a thing apart. It was sheer chance – the fact that the brother of the Royal Naval officer attached to Sandhurst happened to be both the director of human resources in a large company and also a leading light in The Industrial Society – that led to the discovery by the 'outside world' of what I had been up to over a period of five or six years.

Chance also played a hand in getting me out of the Sandhurst 'box'. As I had been adviser on leadership training on an unpaid basis and my contributions had become well received, my request for a sabbatical year to write a book was accepted. I chose to spend it at St George's House in Windsor Castle, a new conference centre for senior leaders in society that had opened its doors in 1966. During my time there I served as its first Director of Studies.

While at Windsor I wrote *Training for Decisions* (Macdonald & Jane, 1969), the book which explored what was being done – and could be done – to train managers to make better decisions, solve problems and to think creatively. In it I introduced the Nine Dots Exercise which, to my surprise, has given rise to a new phrase in the English language – 'thinking outside the box'.

The exercise invited you to connect a square pattern of nine dots with four consecutive lines. The reason why people couldn't solve the problem is that they unconsciously impose a framework on the problem, and try to solve it by drawing the lines *inside* that invisible constraint or 'box'. It is only by starting the four consecutive lines at a point *outside* the box that the problem's simple and elegant solution reveals itself. Hence the phrase 'thinking outside the box' gradually caught on, though most people today are unaware of its origins.

In fact the equivalent *starting point* for the zigzagging growth path of a leader *always lies outside the organization*. That is why leadership development began to look very different to me than the process that was then called 'management development'.

LEADERSHIP OR MANAGEMENT DEVELOPMENT?

The 1960s and 1970s saw the foundation of a number of management colleges in the UK, such as the business schools of London and Manchester. The organization that funded them was the Foundation of Management Education (FME).

At the invitation of Philip Nind, its Director, I talked to the Council of the FME in 1981. Are the business schools developing business leaders? That question has clearly arisen in the minds of some members of the Council. As a result, the FME Council asked me to design and lead a day-long seminar for the heads of the UK's business schools on the subject of leadership development. The seminar took place in October 1982 at the London Business School, with about 100 academics and a few managing directors present. Among them was Dick Clayton, who was responsible for management development in GEC.

I spoke first on the research into leadership. Then I introduced the hourglass model of career change (see page 112) and the 10 principles of leadership development described in summary form as the seven principles of Part 2 of this book. Sir John Harvey-Jones, then Chairman of ICI, next gave an outstanding talk on leadership in management. Edgar Vincent, Group Personnel Manager of ICI, complemented it by describing how ICI was going about the work of developing 'manager-leaders' and changing its organizational culture.

The audience was critical and unresponsive. Travelling back to Waterloo Station on a bus I sat next to a dean of one of the business schools, a long-standing acquaintance who had been at the seminar. She gave me a clue to the audience's relative hostility. 'Your 10 points of leadership development are what we call management development,' she said. It became suddenly clear to me that many business academics were incapable of seeing any need for change, even when they had just heard and seen leadership both eloquently described and exemplified in Sir John Harvey-Jones.

While we were talking *management* the paradigm of 'development' was simple: an organization chose men or women to be managers. If it trained them in management, it either sent them on in-company programmes or public courses. There they learnt the techniques of modern management: knowledge of finance, marketing, techniques for planning and controlling, how to motivate people using the findings of industrial psychology, together with case studies, organizational theory, etc. Attempts to change the personality of the managers – social engineering – were mercifully rare outside the United States. Experiments there with group techniques to change the personality of managers ironically were the same as those that would be used by the Chinese to 'brainwash' US prisoners during the Korean War.

In the 1970s it looked as if leadership training (ACL) could be slotted into that model as *skills* training – wasn't leadership just managing people? Others saw it as an acceptable introduction to the 'behavioural sciences'. But the concept of leadership I had discovered embraced far more than skills. I began to see that it takes a whole society – not just its working 'parts' or organizations – to grow leaders. Therefore my Chair in Leadership Studies had to be set in a university, not a business school.

Methods by which people learn

■ *Teaching*   Applies to any manner of imparting information or skill so that others may learn. It often includes a guided process of assigned work, discipline, directed study and the presentation of examples. It may or may not suggest an academic context.

■ *Training*   Means the systematic development of the body or mind for the purpose of acquiring proficiency in some physical or mental pursuit.

■ *Educating*   Refers in a more general way to a long-range, wide scale, usually academic process. Sometimes the word suggests the accomplishing of greater results than *teach*: schools that teach but simply fail to *educate* their students. It implies attempting to bring out latent capabilities or qualities.

■ *Instructing*   Is mostly restricted to the specific situation of guided training (such as car driving) or the imparting of information or commands. It suggests methodical or formal teaching.

■ *Tutoring*   Is guiding or teaching people individually in a specific subject.

■ *Coaching*   Comes from the image of a tutor conveying a student through a set of examinations as if in a coach or wheeled vehicle. It can either suggest intensive training and the direction of team strategy, as in the field of sport, or else one-to-one tutoring or training.

■ *Mentoring*   Is acting as a trusted counsellor and guide. There may be little or no teaching or learning involved in the conversation.

If we are looking at leadership in the round – what you are and what you believe, as well as the acquisition of skills and technical/professional knowledge – then we are talking *education*. In its formal sense – schools and universities – that sphere, like every other, has undergone massive change since the 1960s. In that decade, for example, in the UK about 10 per cent of young people went to university; now the figure is close to 50 per cent. If it is *society* that grows leaders and not organizations, then an obvious question arises: what are our schools and universities doing – if anything – to educate leaders? What should they be doing?

SCHOOLS FOR LEADERSHIP

The idea that schools are gardens for leadership – the places where seeds are planted and first green shoots spotted, tended and encouraged – is not a new one.

> We are they who help to make or mar all. They that are the flower of our nation, and those who become leaders of all the rest, are committed to our education and instruction.
>
> (John Brinsley, writing to his fellow
> schoolmasters in *A Conclusion for
> Our Grammar Schools*, 1622)

At the root of the great Renaissance schools lay the most characteristic Socratic or Greek concept of leadership, which I could express as: *authority to lead in a free society goes to the one who knows*. By equipping some members of society – ideally chosen solely by aptitude to learn – with the available knowledge and the means to acquire more, schools were in effect teaching their pupils to be leaders. More, by teaching them Latin and (from 1509) Greek, the door was open to a body of writings, such as Xenophon and Plutarch, which was in fact the world's first literature on leadership.

This idea produced fruit in the 19th century, especially among the Renaissance schools that became what the British call public schools – Eton, Harrow, St Paul's, Westminster, Charterhouse, etc. As Gary McCulloch has shown in his academic study *Philosophers and Kings:*

Education for leadership in modern England (CUP, 1991), the 'English tradition' was deeply influenced by Plato's *Republic*:

> Therefore we must elect as ruler and guardian of the city him who as a boy and youth and man has been tested and has come out without strain, and render him honours in life and after death, giving him the highest rewards of public burial and other memorials. The others we must reject.

Plato, you may recall, conceived his ideal society as having three occupational classes – *workers and slaves, guardians* and *philosophers*. In this society the king would draw up the plans and the philosophers would carry them out with the aid of the civil service and military officers comprising the guardian class. Notice this early and partly misleading distinction between *management* and *execution*. Leaders determine the overall plan and infuse the system with a character and direction, then managers direct the workers and slaves to do the work.

To this austere game-plan the British added games of their own, such as cricket, soccer and rugby football. These extraordinary social creations were in fact ways of training team leadership and teamwork while making it fun for boys to learn. Because these games took place outdoors – outside the 'box' of the classroom – boys could both enjoy themselves and learn the Three Circles philosophy without knowing it. (Mike Brearley, one of England's most successful cricket captains, referred to the model in his *Art of Captaincy*, Hodder & Stoughton, 1982.) The Duke of Wellington is once said to have remarked that 'the battle of Waterloo was won on the playing fields of Eton'.

The links between the elite public schools and the principal universities of Oxford and Cambridge, was a close one in this respect. Just as the rapid expansion of the British Army in World War II grew leaders as the opportunities for operational and strategic leadership experience expanded, so the march of the British Empire in the Victorian era grew leaders. Much of the world map was coloured red; there were plenty of chances in the imperial colonies of India, Africa, the Near and Far East to not only lead but lead at the level of Plato's 'philosopher-king' – the strategic-level leader with *phronesis*, or practical wisdom.

These ever-expanding opportunities of leadership in the Empire and the new 'education for leadership' in the elite public and grammar schools produced a flowering of remarkable British leaders across every field of human enterprise – Brunel, Gordon, Kitchener, Churchill, Livingstone, T E Lawrence, Milner, Gladstone, Disraeli, Nightingale, etc.

One such leader, Cecil Rhodes, left in his will in 1902 provision for the foundation of the Scholarships at Oxford that bear his name today. His Scholars were to be elected against certain criteria, carefully proportioned: in every 10 marks they obtain, literary and scholastic achievements would count as three, athletics as two, a specified list of virtues as three, and moral force of character and capacity for leadership as two. Rhodes was clearly attempting to establish an advanced cadre of Empire leaders at Oxford.

In my lifetime the British Empire disintegrated bit by bit, and I was among the last to serve in it as a conscript soldier before the watershed of Suez (1956). In parallel, as McCulloch narrates, the 'English tradition' of education for leadership gradually lost its way: it came to espouse and serve the values of 'competitive individualism'. In 1970, when I was doing research at Oxford, someone sprayed the grey hoardings outside the Sheldonian Theatre with aerosol in white letters a yard high: THE ONLY GOOD LEADER IS A DEAD LEADER.

Yet arguably the tradition did not die, it merely changed its form. R H Tawney, whose lectures at the London School of Economics I heard in 1950, pointed the way forwards in *Education: The task before us* (Workers Educational Association, 1943). 'Democracy,' he wrote, 'needs experts, representatives and leaders; *but it needs them as servants not masters*'. How could the British secondary and higher educational system be oriented towards growing such servant-leaders?

Growing school leaders

The Empire and Platonic vision of leadership education in school and university owed much to a few great educational leaders, such as Thomas Arnold at Rugby and Benjamin Jowett at Balliol College,

Oxford. The key to me seemed to be the headteacher. Having taught briefly in a state secondary school myself in 1960, I had been much impressed by the joint headteachers, a man and woman. Emerson's axiom that 'an institution is the lengthened shadow of one man' has a lot going for it when it comes to schools, much less so at college or university level. If the headteacher is a true leader, I reasoned, at least the staff and pupils will be learning leadership by example.

In 1970 I had an opportunity to explore this territory and in particular to test the concept of the generic role of leader in this field. As head of the Leadership Department at The Industrial Society that year I organized a day-long seminar on the subject, which more than 100 headteachers from both public and private sectors attended. The response was extremely positive, and we then initiated the first-ever series of leadership courses for headteachers, entitled 'Leadership in Schools and Colleges'.

CASE STUDY:
HEADMASTER OF A LINCOLNSHIRE HIGH SCHOOL

I found the two-day course and its one-day follow-up painful, refreshing and inspiring. Painful because it made me realize how haphazard and illogical my previous management style had been; refreshing because it made me re-examine every aspect of my headship; and inspiring because I realized that it was a total philosophy – not something from which one could take ideas in isolation. It has given me a strategy for working instead of my previous hotchpotch of good and bad practice.

First, *thinking time*. I still tend to fill all my time, partly because I am a product of a family background which believed that idleness was synonymous with laziness, but I do deliberately leave my study to walk round the campus, listen to pupils and try to see different aspects of problems. Incidentally, following the ACL practices on delegation seems to have meant that I now get only the difficult problems. I would dearly love to take a lunch break, but that remains a distant prospect in these turbulent times. For thinking time, moments of peace at home have to suffice, but I have come to recognize that thinking time must be found so that I can detach myself for a while and try to take a more distant view of my school. Only then do the really important things emerge and the unimportant ones fade into the background. All headteachers need vision: I do not think it attainable without regular thinking time.

Secondly, *delegation*. I have always found delegation and the involvement of all staff in the task rather elusive – not because I feel threatened, nor because I doubt the abilities of those around me, but because of the difficulty of monitoring and possibly having to pick up the pieces afterwards. Yet the values and importance of delegating are not lost upon me. I have instituted all the machinery for delegation: 1) an Academic Board meeting monthly and advising on all curriculum aspects, 2) an Operational Research Unit of six (myself, two Deputies and three Heads of Year), meeting weekly and examining all aspects of the running of the school, and 3) a daily meeting with my Deputies to prepare for the assemblies and the day ahead.

Departments meet at least once a term: year tutors meet fortnightly; and a weekly bulletin keeps everyone informed of all aspects of school life, yet the one completely democratic forum I keep to a minimum: the Staff Meeting. I found Staff Meetings mentally exhausting and looked upon them as a necessary exercise which rarely simplified or brought inspiration to the school's general aims. We meet as a staff of 50 once a term – more often if necessary – and I now follow ACL advice with care:

■ I prepare the agenda well in advance and publicize it, having invited contributions from all.
■ I make it clear that what I say initially is policy and that what conclusions the meeting may come to later are advisory. I do this because a discussion involving 50 rarely comes to a conclusion of any kind.
■ I arrange seating in a very large circle.
■ I provide free tea and buns.
■ I take Any Other Business items as being items for the agenda of the next meeting.

■ I start on time and specify a finishing time.
■ I chair the meeting and insist on apologies in person to myself.
■ And after my initial input, I leave my deputies to put the hierarchy line, concentrating on directing the discussion, trying to summarize, and trying to select good points to applaud and adopt.

The ACL course brought to me a priceless gift: a means of measuring partial success in influencing and motivating staff. When a breach occurred in relationships, I used to feel that I had failed. Now I can see that breach as a faltering and know that it is part of the continuous process of building the team and of developing the individual. A previously nebulous concept of management has taken on form and structure. I now believe that all members of staff can be influenced and led albeit slowly and probably unwillingly along a road towards a definable goal.

I believe that the ACL training enables a headteacher to fulfil his leadership role with more purpose, more understanding and in a much more structured fashion. It has given me a workable, progressive method of improving my school and I can see that it will continue to stand me in good stead.

In the 1970s these pioneering leadership courses for headteachers touched several hundred in the same way as in the case study above, but there were some 30,000 secondary and primary school headteachers in the UK. My task was to persuade the UK government to adopt a strategy for leadership development. No easy one, for one expensive national 'management development' unit for schools, established in Bristol and staffed by academics, had proved to be useless and collapsed in ignominy.

A report that should have changed that climate and put leadership development for heads on the map was published in 1977 by H M Inspectorate of Schools, entitled *Ten Good Schools*. Having made a list of 50 schools known to be 'good', the Inspectorate selected 10 for diversity and tried to figure out what they had in common. The answer was simple. good schools have good heads. The report characterized them as follows:

> These schools see themselves as places designed for learning; they take trouble to make their philosophies *explicit* for themselves and to *explain* them to parents and pupils; the foundation of their work and corporate life is an acceptance of shared values.
>
> Emphasis is laid on consultation, teamwork and participation, but without exception, the most important single factor in the success of these schools is the quality of *leadership* at the head. Without exception, the heads have qualities of *imagination* and *vision*, tempered by realism, which have enabled them to sum up not only their present situation but also attainable future goals. They appreciate the need for specific educational aims, both social and intellectual, and have the capacity to communicate these to staff, pupils and parents, to win their assent and to put their own *policies* into practice. Their sympathetic understanding of staff and pupils, their acceptability, good *humour* and sense of *proportion* and their *dedication to their task* has won them the respect of parents, teachers and taught. Conscious of the corruption of power and though ready to take final responsibility, they have made power-sharing the keynote of their organization and administration. Such leadership is crucial for success and these schools are what heads and staffs have made them.

'The implication of *Ten Good Schools* is simple,' I wrote in *Developing Leaders* (Talbot Adair, 1988). The secondary educational system in the UK – like the Services, industry or commerce – needs to grow leaders. But developing leaders, as we have seen in Part 1, is more than a matter of organizing courses. It requires a strategy. In fact, weight must be given to each of the 10 principles of leadership development. (In this book I have reduced my original 10 principles to seven, leaving out as separate headings: *Research and Development Adviser*, *Getting the Structures Right*, and *Organizational Climate*.)

Not for another 10 years after 1988, however, would a partnership between the Teacher Training Agency and myself sit down to devise a strategy for leadership training for some 8,000 headteachers in three years, the largest *strategic* approach to developing senior leaders the UK has ever seen. As a result of its outstanding success, the Prime Minister's office found £30 million and the government established a new National College of School Leadership to take on the new programmes and develop the whole field of leadership in schools.

GROWING UNIVERSITY LEADERS

In 1930, the University of St Andrews inaugurated the first of a long series of lectures on leadership, funded by a local family. John Buchan gave the first one, and some 30 lecturers – including Wavell and Montgomery – followed suit. Montgomery was much taken by the experience, and circulated copies of his lecture 'Military Leadership' to all his officers in the British Army on the Rhine. To me, in 1968, he wrote in his even, clear handwriting:

> Leadership is an immense subject. Nowhere is it more important to teach it than at Sandhurst and in our universities; in fact to youth, since it falls on dead ground with the older generation.

In 1983, the university where I held the chair of leadership invited me to speak to the national conference of university secretaries and registrars – the senior administrators – which was taking place there. During my talk I threw out the idea that the time was now ripe for heads of university departments to be taught leadership. The university asked me to run some pilot courses for its own heads, but I insisted on them being open to all universities in order to have more cross-fertilization.

Personally I led 10 of these courses at Farnham Castle in the 1980s, and a further five for vice-chancellors and their senior staff. Then I convened a meeting of the Minister for Higher Education, the Chairman of the University Grants Commission and the Chairman of the Committee of Vice-Chancellors and Principals in order to agree a strategy for leadership development in universities. But like other summit meetings this one proved to be fruitless. Now, some 15 years later, a Universities Leadership Foundation has come into being, which doubtless will come up with the missing strategy.

Still, the team that I had created at Surrey University continued to run leadership programmes based on my work. At one such programme, for heads of colleges and schools, including the large teaching hospitals of the University of London, the Vice-Chancellor – a former Rector of Imperial College named Lord Flowers – had this to say:

> Early in his book, *Effective Leadership*, John Adair quotes a letter that Field-Marshal Viscount Montgomery wrote to him in 1968.
>
> I won't attempt the famous intonation, but I'm sure the rhythm of the sentences will come through: 'Leadership is an immense subject. Nowhere is it more important to teach it than at Sandhurst and in our universities; in fact, to youth, since it falls on dead ground with the older generation.' I will take that as my text.
>
> The more one thinks about Montgomery's assertion, the more extraordinary it becomes. First, of course, there was almost certainly no overt academic teaching of leadership in British universities in 1968. The new universities, together with a few older centres of commercial relevance such as LSE, had barely begun to exert an influence on the system as a whole by their teaching of what might collectively be termed 'management studies'. Business schools were in their infancy: London's was founded in 1965. So the suggestion of teaching leadership ran quite against the academic tide of the late 1960s.
>
> It also ran against the tide of general opinion. Consensus was of course the vogue: nowhere more so than in universities.
>
> If an organization's purpose and its future are linked, then it is not only the present leaders who matter. Indeed, training them in leadership may well be a little beside the point: an old dog may learn an odd new trick, but can rarely change his whole act. We have to look to our leaders of the future. By that, I do not necessarily mean identifying bright individuals in their late twenties who may make it to the top of their institutions – if they stick around for long enough. I mean creating a climate in which leadership can flourish, rather than be restrained by precedent and the safety belt of committee decisions...

I wish to conclude simply by reminding you of the remark of Montgomery with which I began; that it is most important to teach leadership to youth, since 'it falls on dead ground with the older generation'. It may be that our most difficult, yet most vital, challenge of leadership is to prepare the next generation to lead.

May I finish by saying 'Thank you' to John Adair for the extremely important work he is doing for universities in general, and for agreeing to lead this particular study group for our university, which contains many fine leaders, some of whom are in this room tonight, but none who could not learn a little more by contact with their fellows.

To prepare the next generation to lead. If supporting universities – or the vice-chancellor and senior leaders – did begin to interest themselves in that challenge, what would it mean in practice? One reason why I more or less created the Centre for Leadership Studies at the University of Exeter in 1996 was to explore that very question, for there is no one single answer, as I suggested in a public lecture at that university: what is needed is some fundamental and creative thinking – just the sort of thinking, in fact, that universities are in business to do.

NEW OPPORTUNITIES FOR 'EDUCATION FOR LEADERSHIP'?

Passionate as I am about the potential contribution of schools and universities to the education of 'leaders for tomorrow' – the title of my inaugural lecture at Surrey – I remain convinced that *experience* is the watershed in my field, at least from the perspective of teaching leadership. Without experience all the concepts and words remain abstract. Leadership education is essentially adult education.

The real breakthrough in adult *education* for leadership – not *training* – came through my renewed involvement with St George's House in Windsor Castle. As I mentioned, this small institution was set up with two aims in mind: to be a place where senior people in society could meet to discuss important issues, especially of a moral or ethical nature, and to provide further education for the clergy of the Church of England. My task as Director of Studies was to put some intellectual foundations under this work.

What I identified as the key concept was *values*, a word relatively obscure in 1968. It was values that linked the tradition of Christendom with our secular society, including the moral and spiritual values that interwove the very fabric of that society, often beneath the surface, like gold and silver thread. In the context of leadership, values in any field served a different function than vision, purpose or strategy: *it is our values that give us the stars by which we navigate ourselves through life.*

Values, of course, cannot be *trained* for, like skills. We acquire our values, but education gives us the chance to explore, modify, extend or refresh them. *Leadership* is a value – it is part of the value-system of the Services, for example. Why not explore it?

An opportunity came to experiment in this direction. Since moving on from St George's House I have always stayed in touch, and while Charles Handy was Warden, a programme for younger leaders from every kind of organization was instituted. At the first one in 1979 I spoke on leadership, together with the historian Corelli Barnett. Here is what he said.

A HISTORIAN LOOKS AT LEADERSHIP

Given the course of English history, which I see as a quest for liberty, equality and personal responsibility, there is no hope that we will ever become good technological ants, loyal cogs in the organization. We have to find an English road to salvation.

Now earlier in my talk I suggested that in modern industrialized society a leader needed both the raw quality of leadership – personal force and will – *and* complete technical mastery of the job itself. It would seem that British management is too often lacking in both. But then 'leadership' is not much talked about with regard to industry. 'Management' is the preferred word. 'Management studies' thrive. Is there here another source of trouble?

Note the entirely different resonances of these two phrases: 'trade union leaders'; 'plant managers'. Try switching the epithets and you get even more clearly the difference between the resonances of the words: 'trade union *manager*'. How funny it sounds! 'Plant leader' – the same. I think this sharply brings out that management and leadership are not at all the same thing. To my mind 'management' is concerned with the inanimate – material and financial resources, machinery, products, marketing. 'Leadership' is concerned with people; it is a psychological – or if you like, a spiritual – connection between human beings. Therefore, given the historical nature of our industrial population, more emphasis on 'management' and 'management training' will not cure our problems. To think in terms of 'managing' your fellow men is in any case to dehumanize both them and the relationship between you. This is shown by the very jargon of the 'behavioural sciences' – even as white rats.

We must think, then, in terms of 'leadership' – but a form of leadership still new to industry, even though much in the British tradition. The leader not as *boss*, but as first among *equals*; seeking to bring out the full potential of those he works with; careful to carry them with him in all he seeks to do. He will lead not through rank or the weight of social position, but by virtue of superior intelligence and strength of personality; by virtue of being best at the job itself. He will devolve and share responsibility and decision as far as he can. He will need insight into his team mates and their strengths and weaknesses. He will welcome ideas and suggestions from those who in a former dispensation might have been regarded as his inferiors. He will build a relationship of mutual trust.

However, such a style of leadership implies radical changes in the organizational framework of industrial life. For example, the final abolition of those outward forms that proclaim a distinction between boss and man, white collar and blue collar.

It may therefore be that our salvation as an industrial nation, as well as an immense step forward as a society, will lie in the coming at long last to every office and shopfloor of that English habit of cabinet government which first evolved in Downing Street 250 years ago... the free collaboration of *responsible individuals* in a common enterprise.

Corelli Barnett

In the mid-1990s these Windsor Meetings, as they were called, were revived and, with my help, refocused on 'good leadership and leadership for good'. Under the auspices of the Windsor Leadership Trust, six one-week programmes a year are arranged, real opportunities for leadership education. In the 2003 Newsletter of the Windsor Leadership Trust I included these reflections:

When my first book *Training for Leadership* (1968) was published I was living in Windsor Castle as the first Director of Studies at St George's House. It was the only book coming out that year with 'Leadership' in the title: last year there were more than 2,000 such titles, so times have certainly changed.

But have the principles of leadership changed? I don't think so. At the heart of the process is the nuclear reaction of theory or principles on the one hand and practices or experience on the other. It's a two-way process: learning happens when the sparks jump between the two.

Of course it is essential to get the right theory and principles (which is not the latest necessarily, as the newer-is-truer school tends to believe). In my experience far too little though is given to that requirement. I reject the view that it is all subjective: there are some classic and timeless principles of effective leadership at all levels. In a good programme the interaction between theory and practice sets up a chain reaction which is continued as a kind of learning path in the mind of the participant after the course and when faced with the challenges of leading in work.

Although the two overlap, often considerably, there is a useful distinction between *training* and *education*. The former focuses on the systematic development of skills with a specific role in view. The latter is more to do with the whole person and encompasses such areas as values, attitudes, beliefs and ethics. It is long range and wide scale; it implies some attempt to draw out latent capabilities, and it has no specific outcomes in view.

As a general principle, primarily educational programmes like those of the Windsor Leadership Trust should complement leadership training, not replace it. What the Trust can do is to provide the experience of exploring the subject with a broad cross-section of leaders from very different fields, which is an essential ingredient in the educating for leadership process. For it takes people out of their narrow and often uncreative silos and gives them a fresh vision of their field and of themselves. That has been – and is – the Trust's 'unique selling point'. Everything else builds on that foundation.

Yet is there a place for teaching in the sense of the imparting of information about leadership in a more general sense? My honest answer to that question is that you could run a popular and successful programme without such an input. (Not that if I was paying for the people to go on such a programme I would be entirely happy to foot the bill!)

In the WLT context, it is not really a question of what theories, if any, should be taught: that belongs more to the domain of leadership training, where it ought to be an immensely important one. What matters more is that one session on each programme is led by a practitioner, someone who is both well acquainted with the subject and has engaged in some fundamental thinking about it for themselves. They are not parrots of the latest theories or gurus. Such teachers are very hard to come by, and yet without them leadership education at the highest level is scarcely possible.

Such a person may indeed introduce their own tentative conclusions at the right time but their real function is to be a catalyst to help others begin to form their own philosophy or framework of principles, values and policies as a leader or leader-to-be. What they do is help you clarify and deepen your own emerging concept of leadership and fall in love with leadership. Here straight lecturing is unlikely to be effective! When teaching is done it should be virtually invisible.

As one who aspires to excellence in that form of Socratic teaching, I know just how difficult it is and how many are the pitfalls. Occasionally, however, it comes off. After one programme, for example, a participant came up to me and said: 'You did not teach us, nor did we learn. But it became part of me, as if it was my own thoughts'. That's it!

Personally I am extremely grateful to the Trust for giving me the opportunity to teach at what I regard as the highest level of my profession. Not that I have attained that level yet. But I press on with Alexander Pope's words ever before me:

Men must be taught as if you taught them not,
And things unknown propos'd as things forgot.

Key points

- How to grow leaders transcends organizations, for it is society that grows leaders. But because organizations are the beneficiaries of society in this respect, they should take a strong interest in the educational institutions that begin the growth of leaders.
- Therefore wise senior leaders of organizations always think outside the box – about education, about community and society, about the shape of the evolving world.
- Families are one matrix of leadership. Schools and universities are the second nurseries of leaders. They witness the expanding of horizons as young people observe, reflect, practise, experiment, discuss and explore good leadership – and leadership for good.
- Is there a 'window of opportunity' when we acquire our values – the stars by which we steer in life? Maybe the heels of *integrity*, *enthusiasm* and *compassion*, for example, are laid down in those formative years.
- Schools and universities also equip the potential leader with general *knowledge* and the means for acquiring *technical or professional* knowledge later on. Curiosity – the hunger to learn – the ability to think clearly, and the seeds of creativity: such are the legacies of a good education to a leader.

■ A continuing education for leadership in the adult years of working experience is desirable. 'Once learning solidifies,' said A N
   Whitehead, 'all is over with it.'

*Although our view of the most sublime things is limited and weak,
it is a great pleasure to be able to catch even a glimpse of them.*
                                                    Thomas Aquinas

PRINCIPLE SIX

A Strategy for Leadership Development

When it grew too hot for dreamless dozing, I picked up my tangle again, and went on ravelling it out, considering now the whole house of war in its structural aspect, which was strategy, in its arrangements, which were tactics.

T E Lawrence

Effective leadership, I believe, is too important for the present and future success of a business to be left to the human resources department, much as you may love it. It is a core activity to grow leaders. In the next chapter I shall talk to you as the chief executive about what I think you should be doing about it in the sense of leading it from the front. Here I want to focus on just one aspect of what an organization eventually needs to get right – *a strategy for leadership development*.

Strategy, a military word by origin, is hard to define. But, as the words quoted from T E Lawrence above suggest, it is about the *whole* and not the *parts*. Strategy has three hallmarks:

1. *Long-term*   You have to define what longer-term means in your own context, but strategy is seldom about *today*. If it is very short-term it is more likely to be tactical rather than strategic.

2. *Importance*   In business the *urgent* always tends to drown the *important*. A strategic leader's role is to

think ahead, to ensure that your organization knows where it is going. Stay on the bridge; leave the engine room to the engineers.

3. *Multi-component* There is always more than one element in strategy. It is a whole made up of various complementary components.

Of course your organization may not *need* a strategy for leadership development, for it already has excellent business leaders at all three levels. If that is the case then I shall not detain you by asking you to read these next few pages. You can skip this chapter... no, on second thoughts, wait just a moment. Ask your PA to choose the names of any 12 managers at what I call team leadership level, all of whom are under the age of 30 years. Choose them as a representative cross-section of your organization. Then send them the following e-mail or memo.

LEADERSHIP DEVELOPMENT

It has been put to me that (Snail Holdings) should have a strategy for developing leaders. Personally I think that is totally unnecessary, as I have every confidence in the senior managers of this company. Still, what often seems as clear as glass to the eagle may seem as clear as mud to the worm. So, dear Worm, without giving your name, could you please reply with answers to the following questions:

1. Your manager – how does he or she rate on a scale of 1 (poor) to 10 (excellent) as a leader?
2. Now please rate yourself on the same scale.
3. What is your general impression of the quality of leadership in this company?
4. Human Resources tells me that there has been an 'open' strategy for leadership development since my predecessor's time five years ago. Do you know about it?
5. Have you been trained as a team leader?

6. What have you learnt about being a more effective business leader in the last quarter year?

If you would prefer to come and talk to me I would welcome that, for I want to get this decision right. If so, fix a time and date with Mary. Thanks and best wishes.

REVIEWING THE STRATEGY

Thanks to the leadership revolution, it is now probable – at least in the UK – that most organizations will have a plan or strategy labelled 'leadership development'. I suggest you take a careful look at it in the light of this book. Here are some questions to consider:

■ Are there any hidden assumptions? Is the practical philosophy behind it clear? In particular, have the authors a clear idea of what leadership is and how it relates to management? Do they know what it is that we are trying to develop?
■ Does the strategy reflect the principle that no one should be given a leadership role without some form of training, education or preparation for it?
■ A boring point, but what has the strategy cost? What is the over-all amount of money being spent on leadership development? Is the cost per person per day of the team leadership training courses specified? I ask these questions because it is possible to waste thousands of pounds on so-called leadership development.
■ Is the system of line leaders acting as leadership mentors to their apprentice-leaders working effectively?
■ How is the leadership development strategy being evaluated? What are the progress markers?
■ Is too much resource being lavished on too few people at the top?
■ How does the strategy or plan show how we improve our identi-fication of leadership potential in the selection process?
■ What 'research and development' is envisaged in the strategy?

What reviewing the published strategy will tell you is how far the authors have been obeying the injunction *to think and to think until it really hurts.* If you have in your hand a paper that is clear and simple, reasonably short but comprehensive, free of jargon, practically oriented, relevant at every point to your overall business strategy, within budget, intellectually well-founded, and challenging but feasible, then you are a fortunate chief executive. It's not much fun building a house if the architects cannot produce a plan.

GETTING THE STRUCTURES RIGHT

One of your own key functions as a strategic leader is *to balance the whole and the parts* (see page 139). There isn't a formula for doing it; like a helmsman you balance wind and sails in the course, adjusting all the time. But to avoid constant and counter-productive reorganizing, it is worth getting it more or less right. It impinges on your strategy for developing leaders, because if you don't get the roles right your selection and training/education will be confused. Yokes or harnesses (organizations) are supposed to make work easy for oxen or horses, not to chafe, irritate and slow them down.

In political language, the key principle is *subsidiary*: that the whole should not do what the parts can do perfectly well for themselves. The division between the whole and the parts should not be between the chief executive (king) and the operational leaders (robber barons or 'over-mighty subjects'). Operational leaders are members of the strategic leadership team, thus they are as responsible (if not as accountable) for the whole as the chief executive.

The downsizing and de-layering of the large industrial, commercial and public service bureaucracies of the 1980s, together with some judicious reorganizing, has exposed beneath the fat the bare bones of the structure I discerned in 1983 – the basic team, operational and strategic levels of leadership. For example, take the Metropolitan Police in London: Commissioner (strategic) – 32 Borough Commanders (operational) – Police Sergeant (team).

CASE STUDY: OXFORD UNIVERSITY

Who is in the role of strategic leader in Oxford University? Who are the operational leaders and the team leaders? Read this case study and see if you can identify the answers.

Back in the Palaeozoic era when the first tetrapods evolved, natural selection favoured a limb with five digits. This highly successful design was later elaborated by different species in many different ways, including the wonderfully versatile human hand. In 2000, Oxford implemented its decision to organize the academic structure of the University into five subject based divisions.

The new structure grew out of the 'strategic oversight at the centre combined with decision-making devolved to the lowest responsible level'. In contrast, the existing system kept most of the decision-making in the hands of central bodies, particularly the General Board of the Faculties. 'Previously, departments had to relay their thoughts to faculty boards, which relayed them to the General Board,' says Professor Peter Newell, head of the Life and Environmental Sciences Division and himself a former member of the General Board. 'They rarely made a decision straight away, because they had to consult other faculty boards. It all took a long time.'

Under the new structure the General Board no longer exists, and there are faculty boards only for the humanities subjects and for the two social science subjects (law and management) that are not based in departments. Instead, each of the five Divisional Boards has responsibility for coordinating decision-making among its own departments or faculties. In their turn, the departments are encouraged to make their own plans as far as their resources allow. The principal remaining central body is the Council, which confines itself to strategic matters affecting the whole University. All the heads of division have a seat on the Council.

They are unanimous in their view that the new system provides for better and faster decision-making. 'It's a great advantage to plan strategically and think coherently about objectives,' says the head of the Humanities Division.

'The division has a better understanding than the General Board did of what's going on in the faculties.' At the Social Sciences Division, Donald Hay immediately comes up with two examples of projects that have reached fruition during the past year at a speed that would have been unthinkable under the previous system. 'The MSc in Criminology and Criminal Justice was through the system and approved within weeks,' he says. 'And the Oxford Internet Institute – that happened with astonishing speed. There is a sense that we don't have to march off and ask permission for things any more. What we're saying to departments is that if they've got a good reason for doing something and can set it up within the standard structures, they should go ahead and do it.'

If there are differences between divisions, they also have interests in common, and the new structure, far from creating five mini universities, has made it easier for divisions to collaborate. The area where biology and physical sciences meet is one of the hottest in science at the moment, and the science divisions have put a lot of effort into new initiatives such as the interdisciplinary research centre in bio-nanotechnology and new chairs in bioinformatics and chemical biology. 'It's now much easier to make people get together,' says Brian Cantor. 'There are three heads of science divisions and we meet regularly. Under the old system it just wouldn't happen – there were lots of missed opportunities because there wasn't a mechanism.'

(*Oxford Today*, Hilary Issue 2002)

You will notice from this case study that *structure* and *leadership* are closely related to the speed and quality of *decision-making*. If you want your business to be fast on its feet, then you need to get the structure right. One of the largest bureaucracies in history evolved in the Spanish Empire in the 16th century and its slowness in decision-making became proverbial: 'If death came from Madrid we should live forever.'

WHAT SURROUNDS AND INFUSES A SUCCESSFUL STRATEGY IS CULTURE

If you are talking leadership, you are talking integrity – the quality that engenders trust. If a leader proves not to have integrity, then the word *leader* becomes inappropriate. Such a person downgrades himself or herself to being a non-leader or a misleader.

It follows that a culture that in practice does not value integrity – whatever it says in its Corporate Values statement – is a hostile environment as far as growing true leaders is concerned. The trouble is that you can spend years building that reputation for integrity, but it can be lost in a week by some mindless managers. Reputation is a most valuable asset.

In the 1980s I was asked to advise the chief executive of Hambros Bank and his senior team on developing leadership in merchant banking. My 'learning curve' was put to the test, for I knew nothing about merchant banking. I asked for a yardstick of excellence in that field. Two merchant banks were mentioned most frequently as being the best: Warburg's and Morgan Grenfell. What was their secret? Sir Derek Higgs, a senior adviser to UBS Investment Bank, answers the question about Warburg's in a review of a book by Sally Bibb and Jeremy Kourdi, called *Trust Matters*, published in *Management Today* (May, 2004).

CASE STUDY: THE WARBURG SPIRIT

Siegmund Warburg wrote this about the importance of the reputation of a professional services firm. A firm's reputation, he said, 'is like a very delicate living organism which can easily be damaged and which has to be taken care of incessantly, being mainly a matter of human behaviour and human standards'. What he was describing was trust, and it matters.

I was privileged to spend a quarter of a century working in the firm that carried Warburg's name, before I took on the challenge of helping to change the culture and business model of a financial institution of the British old school. The contrast between the two in matters of trust could not have been starker. I doubt the term 'networking' originated in Warburgs, but it felt like it did. Teamwork, the absence of stars and the sharing of information distinguished the firm in every sense. Trust in colleagues was absolute.

I had never heard the term 'silo' before I joined the financial institution. But I soon learnt that its culture was the antithesis of what I had grown up with and learnt to respect at Warburgs. Knowledge kept to oneself was power over others. Baronies, fiefdoms and self-promotion ruled. Doors were, literally and metaphorically, closed, not open...

There is nothing fundamentally objectionable or mistaken about this book. Indeed, it's a worthwhile reminder of bedrock values. But if you want prose that lifts off the page and tells you about the human spirit and its capacity to trust, this is what Siegmund Warburg wrote to George Bolton in 1950 when the latter was knighted.

'You deserve it above all for your single-minded courage in facing the truth, however hard and unpalatable; in giving due consideration not only to the bigger and self-evident matters, but also to the smaller and intricate things, which so often add up to big issues; in always taking the strenuous road rather than the way of least resistance; and above all in always fighting for the cause you consider right, however hard it may be.'

Questions:

■ What three words would you use to describe the culture of Warburgs?
■ Do you think good teamwork makes a difference in merchant banking?
■ How did Siegmund Warburg exercise strategic leadership?

In the case of Warburgs, the person who set up the company also established an acceptable set of ground rules – a way of operating that everyone can work with – a way in which they like working. Great companies have a sound in the woodwork that was put in by the founder that sustains them.

Strategic thinking, then, about growing and sustaining true leadership is much more than a paper strategic plan for leadership courses or programmes. Paper plans are easy. What is harder to achieve is a culture change in this context: a liberating and empowering structure – one in which those in leadership roles are free to take decisions, to develop their potential and to work creatively with others. Add to that a climate of hope, confidence and commitment – so that every manager is ready to seize the opportunities on offer – and you are getting closer to the summit of Everest. Keep going.

Key points

■ There are many ways an organization can help a person grow as a business leader, some of them necessary conditions – such as chances to lead, training and line leaders whom they can respect and learn from – and others that are more 'optional extras'.

■ The *whole* is always greater than the *parts*. If the various parts of leadership development – for example, selection and training or education – work together in harmony in a strategic approach, then the end result is going to be that much greater. 'If you miss them on the swings, you catch them on the roundabouts.'

■ Look on *structure* as part of your overall leadership development strategy, giving as much freedom in decision-making to your business leaders as you possibly can within the constraints of your business. Expect them to work creatively together as a team, and in turn to give *their* team leaders as much discretion as they can. Responsibility grows leaders.

■ We know that moral values are intrinsic to leadership simply *because human nature is intrinsically good* – not as good as it should or could be, but good. If a chief executive turns his back on truth and slights goodness – in other words, if he abandons integrity – then that organization will stunt leaders rather than grow them.

■ The best leaders have a habit of wanting to work for the best organizations. Why? Because they want to grow. Aim to be the best
organization in your field, the employer of first choice.

*Everyone knows at any given moment who is the best company in its
field. Not necessarily in terms of size or profits, though it could be. I
mean the best in bringing in new products, market sensitivity, presence, range, quality, how we deal with our people, ethical, environmental and safety standards – all of these things.*

Sir John Harvey-Jones

PRINCIPLE SEVEN

The Chief Executive

Power is actualized only when word and deed have not parted company.
Hannah Arendt

Where the top strategic leader is not involved in or committed to the work of developing leadership, in my experience, you may as well forget it. Turning that negative experience into a positive principle:

Principle Seven: An organization that grows leaders is one where the chief executive leads the process from in front.

You will notice that I have used *chief executive*, a title of US origin, in that statement. Titles come and go. I am thinking more in terms of *roles*. You will have to determine who has the top strategic leader role in your organization. It may be the Archbishop of Canterbury or the Prime Minister. Or it may be shared between two people, as in the characteristic British company governance, where the constitution stipulates both a chairman (full-time or part-time) and chief executive/managing director.

The textbook example of a chief executive who exemplified Principle Seven is Sir John Harvey-Jones, and if you want a case study of how he did it in ICI during the 1980s you cannot do better than read his own account in *Making It Happen* (HarperCollins, 1988). Incidentally, he was both the chairman and the chief executive of ICI at the time.

There are pros and cons for having a single top strategic leader. It is a strong leadership position, and in times of crisis the right leader can make the right things happen comparatively quickly. That is why democracies elect virtual dictators in times of crisis (and sometimes have difficulty getting rid of them when the crisis has passed). Yet to appoint a non-leader or a misleader to such a strong leadership position is to court disaster – you shouldn't have much difficulty of thinking of examples, for there is a dearth of leaders at top strategic level in politics, business, public services and churches or faith-communities. As the Hebrew proverb says, 'When the shepherd is angry with his sheep he sends them a blind guide.' Woe to your organization if it has created a strong leadership position and installed a morally blind guide in it.

LEARNING TO BE A TOP STRATEGIC LEADER

The general hypothesis I work on is that there are no bad strategic leaders, only bad teachers of leadership.

In other words, most strategic leaders fall short of the generic role's requirements not out of ill will, nor because they lack the potential, but because they are simply ignorant of their *leadership* role. No one has ever taught them. You can see that I am back to the old song I sang under Principle One, but I am now applying it to the top strategic leader role.

Who might such a teacher of leadership at this level be? In an ideal world it would be someone who has done the job – a Harvey-Jones – and someone who understands leadership theory, for we know that not all good practitioners of an art can teach it. Leonardo da Vinci did not take apprentices, and Mozart had no time in his short life to teach other composers.

Thus the paragon of my trade is Xenophon, who graduated from Socrates' master-class on leadership at the age of 25, a year later became one of the most famous generals in Greek history, and then through his books taught leadership to Alexander the Great, Scipio Africanus, Cicero, Julius Caesar and – in our own age – Lawrence of Arabia.

Some early experiments

Without Xenophon's unique qualifications I found myself in his sandals as the world's first Professor of Leadership Studies. If I did not tackle the problem of training strategic leaders, who else would?

The difficulties were formidable. As Montgomery had warned me in his usual black-and-white and no-nonsense way, remember that leadership *falls on dead ground with the older generation*.

The *older generation* are reared on the milk that *leaders are born not made*. They confuse the two senses of leadership: because they are in the *role* of leader – people called them the leaders in their field – they assume that they must have the *attribute* of leadership. If not, then it can hardly matter. They are already in the job and enjoying its rewards and privileges. Leadership is hardly important, they say, if we got to the top without it.

One solution is to catch people before they become the *older generation* and to give them an opportunity to think about leadership at the strategic level at a point where they had sufficient experience but before they are committed. The prospect of promotion has to be in sight, say within five years.

In 1969, while still Director of Studies at St George's House, I persuaded the bishops of the Church of England to identify and nominate 20 men in the 35–40 age range who had the potential to be senior leaders. Then I designed and led a four-week course for them (see my *The Becoming Church*, SPCK, 1976). Two-thirds of the alumni did become bishops, archdeacons or deans.

My second experiment was to run a leadership course for people who were already in the role of strategic leader. The story (from *Developing Leaders*, Talbot Adair, 1988) was as follows:

> In 1986 two chief executives wrote to me for information about leadership seminars for them. Conscious of the total lack of provision in this area – the core of their role – I tried without success to persuade British institutions, such as the Manpower Services Commission and the National Economic Development Organization, to take up the challenge. For various reasons all declined. Therefore in 1986 I decided to go it alone and lay on such a course myself. (I learnt subsequently that 'course' was the wrong word to use. Like 'training' it smacked of too

low a level. 'Seminar' or 'conference', I was told, are words – like 'development' – that are more acceptable to senior people.)

The course was entitled 'Leadership for Chief Executives' and it took place at Nuneham Park near Oxford. The brochure defined the aim as follows:

'The course is for chief executives, especially those within two years of appointment. Those shortly to become chief executives are also eligible for it.

'The aim of the course it is to provide course members with the opportunity to study the nature and practice of good leadership in order to become more effective in their roles as chief executives.

'The seminar is designed for a small number of individuals drawn primarily from industry and commerce. It will be highly participative.'

The course lasted for a day and a quarter. (Earlier that year I had tried to mount a two-and-a-half days programme for chief executives without success.) The participants arrived in time for introductions over dinner, followed by a session working in pairs and in plenary on the question 'What is the role of a chief executive?' During the following day we explored the chief executive's major areas of leadership responsibility, such as strategic thinking and corporate planning, communication in large organizations, encouraging innovation and enterprise, the 10 steps of leadership development (as in Part 1), and effective time management.

The course was marketed by sending a letter and brochure to the chairman or managing director of the top 600 companies in *The Times* list. About 200 companies replied. Of those who expressed interest the relatively short notice (about four months) ruled out some who were evidently keen to come. Some applicants fell more into the category of senior managers and so I had to decline to accept them. Ten chief executives signed up for the course, although in the end two dropped out at the last moment due to business pressures. Those who came were in charge of major industrial and commercial enterprises, such as ICI's Paints Division and a large City firm of chartered accountants.

Beyond the letters I received after the course I have no means of evaluating this programme beyond my own judgement. One must be sceptical about what any seminar lasting little more than a day can achieve in terms of changing attitudes and imparting skills, but the participants clearly found it valuable to compare notes with their peers, with someone like myself acting more as a catalyst than as teacher or instructor.

In fact I did not repeat the Nuneham experiment, partly because I was a freelance at the time and had no secretary. I needed a partner organization. But the CBI and Institute of Directors, when approached, proved to be uninterested. The Civil Service had just launched its own four-week Top Management Programme – the architect of it, John Mayne, consulted me and I tried to persuade him to call it leadership rather than management, but he told me that leadership was an unacceptable word in Whitehall. But in my view, programmes like the TMP are simply too long. Even the five-day leadership programme run by the British Institute of Management and some business schools struck me as too long. As I wrote in 1988:

> The main point is that a five-day course effectively rules out those who are already chief executives. Instead of being programmes designed for the top person, or those soon to be in the top job, these business school-type courses tend to attract senior managers, more at the operational than the strategic level.

In 2002 I proposed to the Windsor Leadership Trust a partnership in order to run together some three-day programmes for newly appointed strategic leaders. As the series at St George's House develops, it is now clear that the essential ingredients of its success are three-fold:

1. A cross-section of newly appointed strategic leaders from a very wide range of organizations in the public, private and voluntary sectors. This factor induces participants to think generally about leadership, as well as a richer sharing of experience.
2. Three case studies, as I call them: three strategic leaders from different fields talking about their concept of leadership and how they exercise it.
3. One or two sessions with thinkers in the field, including one with me in the generic role of a strategic leader. My *Effective Strategic*

Leadership (Pan, 2001) serves as the intellectual framework for the programme.

The Windsor Leadership Trust programmes are experimental by nature – none of the speakers or facilitators is paid – and a capacity of about 40 participants a year isn't going to change the UK, let alone the world. But what we have established is both that it can be done and how it should be done. In 20 years time it will be inconceivable throughout the world – or much of it – that a person steps up to the level of being a strategic leader without a similar form of specific preparation for the role.

WHAT DOES A STRATEGIC LEADER HAVE TO DO?

In this section I am concerned with only one generic function – the seventh one – of a strategic leader, the one to do with selecting and developing both today's leaders and leaders for tomorrow. It is the one that Jack Welch famously spent about 50 per cent of his time doing during the last years of his long tenure as chief executive of General Electric.

Fortunately, in order to be the teacher-in-chief of leadership in your organization, you only have to do one simple thing: *lead by example*. In Shakespeare's words, it is as if the organization is looking up to you and saying:

> Do not like some ungracious pastors do,
> Show us the steep and thorny way to heaven,
> While he himself the primrose path of dalliance leads,
> And recks [takes] not his own rede [advice].

It is simple but not easy. If it is any encouragement to you, I find it the hardest part of leadership. It is easy to write books on the subject, especially if you have a ready pen, but very hard to practise what you preach to others. But, as they say in examinations, *all candidates must attempt this question.*

For example, take Principle Three. I expect top strategic leaders to make time to spend with each individual of their senior team. This doesn't always happen. Cabinet ministers, for instance, in Margaret Thatcher's government told me that they seldom, if ever, had one-to-one meetings with the Prime Minister.

The content of those meetings will be business. But they create a framework for acting as a leadership mentor, provided there is an openness and willingness to learn – it takes two to tango. But do you want to employ people these days at strategic/operational level who have closed minds on the subject of leadership? People with closed minds become like 'green-mantled stagnant pools'.

If you have the leadership framework or practical philosophy that I have taught you in this book in mind, you will find yourself becoming aware of what an operational leader is *not* telling you, or *not* doing. You may notice, for example, that they are not getting their teams together, not spending time agreeing targets with individuals and reviewing progress, not finding time to think, not avoiding micro-management by delegating, not getting out of their office more than the token one-day-a-week formula.

All teaching at this level is conversational. In such a dialogue, as I have suggested already, the distinction between teaching and learning is blurred. *Qui docet discit*, Seneca said, 'Even while they teach men learn.' Your operational leaders are also your teachers. Find out what they have to teach you, and learn from them. By doing so, if it doesn't sound too paradoxical, you will be teaching them. Of course, like Socrates, you should be able to ask a few questions in order to help the other person to know what he or she knows and does not know – even if they think they do. That is the first pillar in the seven-pillared house of wisdom.

You will start off, for example, not knowing how to be a leadership mentor to your senior operational leaders, or if they will accept you in that function. Do you, you wonder, have that kind of moral or personal authority? You won't know until you try. If you fail, then you mustn't expect others to succeed. Say goodbye to your senior operational leaders acting as leadership mentors to *their* operational/team leaders. If you can't do it, how can they?

Exercise

Take a list of your senior strategic leaders and draw two columns beside it. In one column put down the leadership lessons that you would dearly like to teach that particular individual. In the second column, write the lessons that this leader has to teach you and his or her colleagues.

Remember that if your senior operational leaders – your team – are spending £1,000 a day of the shareholders' money to go to see a personal leadership mentor, thereby wasting both time and money, it is not their fault but yours – you are not doing the job you are paid to do.

MAKE YOUR PRESENCE FELT IN TRAINING FOR LEADERSHIP

You delegate training team leaders to others to organize, manage and lead, but Principle One still falls within your responsibility. By visiting courses you endorse with your presence – and perhaps a few words – the value, worth-whileness, importance of the course and of effective leadership for your company. And you encourage the trainers who, oddly enough, are human and – like all of us – need encouragement.

These 'few words' may get extended to a brief talk on leadership. If it arises naturally – if your own organization invites you to speak on the subject, or on an occasion that allows you to do so – seize it as a rare opportunity to perform your function as teacher-in-chief of leadership. Don't do it too often, however, so that you have a set speech, for scarcity gives value and weight to your words. Everyone knows that you are being paid to lead, not as a speaker on leadership. It is sometimes much more effective to talk briefly about leadership, purpose and values, when your audience are least expecting it, say when you are outlining to the top team or a large gathering of managers the strategic plan for the next three years.

Training courses or leadership education events, however, do provide you with a natural context. On page 22 I quoted the Queen's address at Sandhurst on leadership. That is a model for you. The Queen is head of the Services. Everything is delegated. To Sandhurst is delegated the task of training military leaders. Yet the Queen has not disappeared from the picture. The annual Sovereign's Parade symbolizes her ownership of it in the headship role. In 1966 she came in person and *taught* leadership herself in the address. That is your role in relation to all the team leadership training that is happening – or will be happening – in your organization.

CASE STUDY: THE THOMSON ORGANIZATION

Roy Thomson – Lord Thomson of Fleet – was not only a great business leader but also, as his autobiography *After I Was Sixty* (Hamish Hamilton, 1975) reveals, a great mentor of business leaders. One of them I interviewed for research purposes – his successor Sir Gordon Brunton. He in turn became one of the first advocates of growing leaders rather than training managers. In 1982 Brunton had this to say to his group's human resources conference:

> It is very important that we distinguish between leadership and authority. The acceptance of leadership is almost certainly a voluntary act of those who are led to those who lead. The exercise of authority is outside the realm of persuasion and is concerned with the exercise of power. Leadership has authority and power but authority does not necessarily have leadership.

> Over many years now I have observed with enormous interest, in fact almost with a sense of fascination – and I have been privileged to do so – those who hold very high positions in government and the trade unions, in business and in industry, and very many of them, indeed I would say the majority, have very great authority but they are not leaders.

> Let me now come closer to home and talk about Thomson's. Leadership is the most vital ingredient for our future growth and our future development. We have deliberately chosen a strategy that is based upon leadership and on talent and the success of our policy and, indeed, the very policy itself, depends upon our ability to develop the various levels of leadership.

In saying that I think we must recognize the difference between management and between leadership. Leadership is obviously concerned with management but there are managers who are not leaders. I think one of the important differences is that a manager, particularly a functional manager, is and will continue to be involved in a specific sector or in a particular discipline, but to the leader there are no boundaries; he cuts straight across them either by sector or by company.

This company has grown and has prospered from an entrepreneurial tradition of leadership and of management. Hopefully, that will be as great an asset in the future as it has been in the past but that is by no means certain. It is to find the leaders and the entrepreneurs of the future that we have set up the Strategic Managers Course and if, out of those 15 people who are the top future talent of the organization as we discern it today, we can find one or two or three who can become leaders and entrepreneurs in the terms that I have tried to describe, then I think that our strategy in the years ahead will be in safe hands. If we can't then what we must do is to settle and develop a different strategy because it is those leaders who will make what we are currently trying to do possible. In terms of strategy 10 years is not a long period of time...

Although I could pick Gordon Brunton up on one or two points, this talk is a model for what any chief executive might say on such an occasion. Here are the ground rules:

■ Keep it simple, clear and concise – don't ramble.
■ Avoid jargon such as action-centred leadership, functional leadership, situational leadership, transformational leadership, emotional intelligence, distributive leadership, etc. There may be someone in the audience who knows what it actually means!
■ Avoid telling the story of your life, how you feel, or saying what a miserable worm you are as a leader. The audience hasn't come to hear your war stories. How you are feeling is irrelevant to them, it is what you are *doing* that matters. They are fully aware

that as a leader you are a miserable worm – we all are. 'Remember you are a worm, Winston,' Violet Bonham-Carter once said. Churchill looked dejected, then chuckled and said: 'Yes, I am a worm but at least I am a *glow worm*.' This occasion is a chance for you to glow.

■ Speak without notes – you are singing your own song.

■ Relate what you say about effective leadership to the business, and especially to what strategic direction it needs to take. It gives the relevant context to the critical business of releasing the corporate creative energy within people – the true human resource – needed to achieve the vision.

■ End on an inspiring note. In 2004, Roy Gardner of Centrica sounded the right note in these words:

> There has never been a more challenging time for those of us in business. The challenges will become tougher still, but along with challenge comes opportunity. For those companies that are able and willing to adapt, it's going to be an exciting time.
>
> The world changes quickly and you have to change with it. Sometimes this means thinking about things in a different way. *Looking for the opportunity in everything*, even when it's not obvious. I think that's one thing that distinguishes the leader from the manager.

The important point is that you don't have to be a great orator. Nor do you have to talk a lot of theory about leadership – leave that to the academics. Keep it simple, speak from the heart, don't give the impression either of complacency or arrogance, and make it clear that this is about where you intend to take the business.

One last personal tip from my own experience. If you are a newly appointed strategic leader and you are asked to speak on leadership for the first time over dinner to your senior colleagues, many of whom will be older, more experienced and longer in service than you, you face a challenge. You may find yourself tempted to fortify your spirits by drinking more than your usual gin and tonic. But bear in mind the disastrous example of Mark Twain...

Mark Twain was once invited, as the guest of honour, to a dinner at which all the great leaders of the American Civil War were present. When it came to the speeches the military leaders made their rather lengthy and somewhat heavy remarks. In due course Mark Twain was called on to speak and he rose – a shade unsteadily – to his feet.

'Gentlemen,' he said, 'Caesar is dead; Hannibal is no longer with us; Napoleon has long since passed away; and Wellington is under the sod.

'And – to tell you the truth – I am not feeling too good myself.'
And with that he sat down.

Key points

- If you are in the top strategic leadership role in an organization, you own the problem of selecting and developing the business leaders it needs, not just for today but also for tomorrow. You can share it with others and delegate certain aspects to others, but you are accountable.

- The absolute minimum you have to do is to lead from the front, or lead by example. Bad example shouts. People don't notice good example, for they are expecting it and no special credit attaches to it – it is what your position requires. But it teaches at a subliminal level, unknown to you. 'Example is the school of mankind,' said Edmund Burke, 'and they will learn at no other.'

- Exemplify Principle Three – be a leadership guide and counsellor to your top team *individually*. If you cannot do it, don't expect them in turn to do it to *their* leaders.

- At this level words like *teaching, learning, mentoring, coaching* or *counselling* are best forgotten. A discussion is a conversation with a purpose. The generic agenda – the right questions to ask – are: how are we doing on the common task; how can we (this organization) work better as a *team*; and, how can each *individual* – including you and me as senior leaders – contribute better to the common good?

- Under the headings of Principles One and Two, make your presence felt at the training of team leaders level and at any other corporate leadership education event, and participate personally in selecting leaders for senior appointments.

■ Seize any natural opportunities 'to say a few words' about leadership in face-to-face contexts. E-mailing or faxing your thoughts doesn't count, for paper doesn't communicate. The spirit of leadership that you wish to convey depends upon your presence.

Setting an example is not the main means of influencing another, it is the only means.

Albert Schweitzer

Conclusion

'The grand aim of all science,' said Albert Einstein, 'is to cover the greatest number of empirical facts by logical deduction from the smallest number of hypotheses or axioms.'

For any thinker this statement of Einstein's sets a high standard. In Part 1 I have shared with you my quest – the personal odyssey – for the truth about leadership. I was lucky enough to discover through the Group or Functional Approach the generic role of leadership, the heart or core of the matter. The other two main theories or approaches – the Qualities and Situational Approaches – simply fell into place. Like the pieces of a jigsaw puzzle, the whole picture appeared for the first time in human history – a very exciting moment.

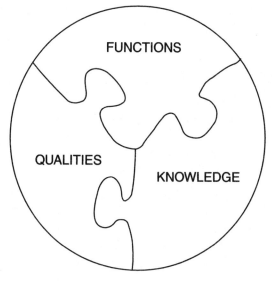

The elements of identity

'There is nothing as practical as a good theory,' said Kurt Lewin. Putting it slightly differently, if a theory or philosophy doesn't *work* when applied to such practical purposes as selection or training, its credibility has to be questioned. The integrated concept of leadership outlined in Part 1 has been put to work in both those domains and has met all the criteria of success and, moreover, it has done so for over 60 years. If there were any other theories or philosophies about leadership that met these stringent criteria I would have included them in this book, but I have found no other that meets Einstein's criteria: *Truth is what stands the test of experience.*

The theme of this book is how leaders – those with leadership potential – grow as leaders. What is clear is that, initially at least, a person acquires leadership like a first language. Such people learn most when they seem to learn least, as if by an unconscious taking-in of knowledge.

Practical experience is the only path. Here learning is by trial and error. As one young National Theatre director said:

> In the undergraduate theatre scene you can spend three years in rehearsal, produce truly terrible shows, and nobody ever tells you never to darken the stage again. If you're smart, you can carry a secret catalogue of your mistakes from show to show, and get a little better at avoiding them. You emerge with confidence to say 'I'm a director' and you keep on saying it till someone believes you.

It takes a similar process to be able to say 'I'm a leader' in any field. The real issue is whether or not we can work with that natural grain. Can we improve on it? Can we cut down the time it takes to reach that first stance on the climb?

The 'we' here has to be split into two questions: what can an individual do to grow as a leader? *and* what can an organization do to grow leaders? But that distinction is still rather artificial. You can't really become an operational or strategic leader outside the context of an organization. Equally, organizations can't find individual people to fill these roles who are not on an inner journey of growing as leaders. *The wings carry the bird; the bird carries the wings.*

No individual leader should ever *depend* upon an organization to school him or her in leadership. With the odd exception of places like

Sandhurst, organizations are not set up to be schools of leadership. Therefore it isn't surprising if they either don't attempt to develop their leaders or if they do, they do it badly or in an intellectually incoherent way.

In fact there is quite a lot that an individual can do *outside* his or her organization – in spite of it – to grow as a leader: for example, community experience, reading and thinking about the subject, and observing good and not so good leaders.

Indeed, it is primarily *society* that grows leaders, not the organizations within it. They are like customers buying either raw materials or half-finished goods. Consequently, a society gets the leaders it deserves. As the Arabic proverb says, 'As you are, so will be the rulers that rule you.' As Tacitus once said: 'Rome being great, deserved great leaders.'

Yet organizations within that social economy do have their own vital part to play. They need to develop leadership for their own ends, and – if they have their wits about them – they need to do it at all levels. This book is what the Romans called a *vade-mecum*, a handbook carried on a person for organizations on how to do it. As organizations cannot read or think, I have taken the liberty of talking to you directly.

Leaders don't grow without inspiration. The path is steep, the load gets heavier, and the slips and falls are more frequent. What may inspire you to go on is having a vision or sense of purpose. Maybe, too, you have a vision of the greatness in your people and what a privilege it is to serve them as their leader. As John Buchan incomparably said, 'The task of leadership is not to put greatness into people, but to elicit it, for the greatness is there already.'

Within the story of leadership development in modern times I have woven into it some threads of my own personal odyssey, as I don't expect to come this way again. I have freely shared with you all that I have learnt. We have shared the story of leadership together and now our paths part. Let me leave you with some words borrowed from a 17th-century German poet:

Friend, you have read enough.
If you desire still more,
then be the odyssey yourself
and all that it stands for.

Index

Also available from Kogan Page

BY THE SAME AUTHOR

Decision Making and Problem Solving

Develop Your Leadership Skills

The Inspirational Leader: How to motivate, encourage and achieve success

Leadership and Motivation

Leadership for Innovation

Not Bosses But Leaders: How to lead the way to success
3rd edn

For these titles and many more, visit the Kogan Page website at www.kogan-page.co.uk

The above titles are available from all good bookshops. For further information, please contact the publisher at the address below:

Kogan Page Ltd
120 Pentonville Road
London N1 9JN
United Kindgom
Tel: +44 (0) 20 7278 0433
Fax: + 44 (0) 20 7837 6348

Order online at:
www.kogan-page.co.uk